The Thai Jack The Ripper

Barbara Hutton

Published by Trellis Publishing, 2021.

While every precaution has been taken in the preparation of this book, the publisher assumes no responsibility for errors or omissions, or for damages resulting from the use of the information contained herein.

THE THAI JACK THE RIPPER

THE THAI JACK THE RIPPER

BARBARA HUTTON

Somkid Pumpuang

Thailand's lush beaches and exotic holiday resorts often perfectly hide the depravity that befalls the local poor population of the country. Hidden in the shadows of explicit beauty, lurks an underworld of forced labor and crimes that go unnoticed and unpunished.

For Somkid Pumpuang, this type of environment lent itself blissfully to his monstrous killing spree.

Due to Thailand's vast lands and poverty-stricken provinces, this monster was able to vent his uncontrollable temper and incessant need for money and lust on the poorest of victims.

Women who often worked in the sex trade out of necessity rather than choice, made them easy targets for Somkid. Often married with children of their own, their only crimes were that they were the only bread winners in their families.

With jobs and education not readily available, the curse of having good looks somehow opened up the unsavory chance to get out of a never-ending rut. Mothers, daughters, wives whose husbands had uncontrollable drug habits to support, or just women who strived for more in their lives, now had a means to affording food on the table for their dependents.

This is the real-life sickening story of one man who prayed on women promising more to them and perhaps, a way out of poverty.

With his grooming techniques, charisma and the promise of wealth and a more secure future, Somkid would spin his tailored solutions to befit their dreams and desires. Incredibly distasteful and a true narcissistic psychopath, Somkid would go wholly unnoticed for a long time before his crimes were eventually unearthed, bringing about not only a global media frenzy, but utter disgrace to himself and everything his country stood for.

Somkid Pumpuang was born in 1964 in Thailand. Due to the untimely death of his parents at just aged five years old, he was taken into the care of his Uncle, Kling Kingkaew who adopted him as one of his own.

But Somkid was always a troubled child, recalls his uncle, remembering him being very bad tempered if things didn't go his way. He was also a troublemaker leading to him eventually being kicked out of school for stealing. But expulsion from school brought no shame to Somkid's demeanor - he just didn't seem to care.

And, despite his uncle managing to secure Somkid a position at a local wood factory, it wasn't long before he was fired from his apprentice job for stealing money.

Somkid's increasingly frequent petty crimes eventually led to more sinister activities, such as drugs and weapons trading in the eastern areas of Thailand. And, simultaneously, his narcissistic side was growing ever more refined allowing him to effortlessly give false testimony in court on an occasion when he managed to frame a local businessman resulting in the accused receiving a six-year prison sentence.

Soon after though, Somkid would serve time in prison himself for committing robbery, and would be sentenced to just four years for his crimes. On his release though, Somkid had somehow masterfully crafted a new reinvented persona for himself during his time in jail. A dominant manipulator now, Somkid would begin to enjoy playing different characters and roles, directing and starring in his own fictitious story, stealthily drawing in the meek and vulnerable for his own sadistic pleasure and gain.

Somkid was to use many aliases, portraying himself as a wealthy businessman; dealer of precious stones and even as a scout for the record industry. Evolving into a man who enjoyed the finer things in life, staying in luxury hotels, Somkid's charismatic charm afforded him many women admirers. His aloof nomadic existence and use of false names was to lead him to his next chapter life. To kill.

On the night of the 30th January 2004, Somkid booked himself into a high-end business hotel in the Mukdahan Province – checking-in under his actual name for a change. He decided to visit a bar called the Sang Tawaen Café Mukdahan, taking a hotel security guard with him to seek out an escort for his evening entertainment.

Whilst there, he watched and listened as Warunee Phimphabut, a twenty-five-year-old lounge singer finished her last few songs. He was immediately taken with her and invited her to join the two men at their table. The owner of the bar, Imchit Paklua overheard the couple happily laughing and chatting together and so, thought nothing more of the situation. Even when her employee, Warunee was leaving to join Somkid for dinner, Imchit felt confident that all was well.

Back at his hotel room, Somkid and his companion ordered room service that evening and, on the following mourning, Somkid woke early and left the hotel.

At 9am the hotel maid entered the now supposed vacant room of Somkid and found a young woman lying face down in the bath. The Mukdahan Police were called straight away by the terrified staff member. An autopsy was performed on the victim who was found to have been aggressively strangled; tied by her ankles and wrists with cable and had died from affixation and then drowned.

Warunee's manager later confirmed that Somkid had in fact told her he was a talent scout from Bangkok, and that with his help, he could make Warunee a famous singer.

Warunee was the only member of her family to have a source of income. She looked after her five younger siblings, not only providing for their everyday needs, but also taking them on their daily 5km journey to school.

On June the 2nd 2005 Somkid was to kill again.

Thirty-four-year-old Pongphan Sabchai, was hired as a personal escort by Somkid for three days. She in fact was a qualified masseuse and also, two months pregnant.

Pongphan too, was found by a hotel maid the following morning in Somkid's hotel room in Lapang. She had also been violently strangled to death and found face down in the bathtub.

This time however, Somkid had used a false name to check in and again left early in the morning, claiming on his hotel booking form that he was a travel executive. He did not leave empty handed though, stealing his victim's rings and cell phone as well as the cash Pongphan had in her purse.

On June the 11^{th,} in Trang Province, Somkid booked into the Charosensri Grand Royal Hotel. This time he was recorded on the hotel's CCTV surveillance system, with his next soon-to-be victim following him into the lift.

Patcharee Amatanirum aged 38, was yet another masseuse that Somkid had smoothly conned into thinking that he was a wealthy Gem Dealer who held the key to changing her life.

This time however, Somkid's behavior was more intense; more desperate and indeed, much more violent.

His victim was again strangled; tied around the ankles and her mouth taped to muffle her screams of desperation. And, for the third time, to finish off his torturous acts, he drowned her in his hotel bathroom as part of his now recurring ritual.

Somkid did not bother to cover his tracks this time, fleeing the scene of the murder after stealing Patcharee's gold jewelry. His psychotic manner meant he no longer cared. He felt a narcissist power within that fed his belief he could do whatever he wanted with no consequences and no remorse.

Somkid now, had three separate police provinces looking for him - Murkdahan, Udon Thani and the Lampany districts. A national manhunt for the gruesome killer was underway and, police felt confident of his imminent arrest having now identified him from hotel CCTV footage. The case was eventually sent to Bangkok where a special task force within the Royal Thai Police was set up under the leadership of police colonel, Chadchai Liamsanguan.

Chadchai recognized his grisly murderer almost immediately. He recalled his run-ins with Somkid during an investigation he led into fraud several years earlier. Digging out the 5-year-old mugshot of his culprit, scanning all the available CCTV footage and, sending the handwriting samples gleaned from various hotel booking forms, Chadchai knew he had his man.

As if wishing to be acknowledged, Somkid had in fact, been quite aware of the CCTV cameras within the hotels he frequented. Bowing his head in shoots caught near hotel entrances and when entering and existing the lifts, Somkid had teased his existence and his crimes to the unsuspecting hotel staff and police.

Now with his photo aired on news channels all over Thailand and in the press, hotels, bars and massage parlors were put on full alert and informed to watch out for this dangerous murderer and to immediately report any sighting of him to police authorities.

Unfortunately for two more women, this information and, Somkid's eventual arrest, came too late.

Porntawan Pungkhabut was to be Somkid's fourth victim and the third to take place in the month of June.

Porntawan was a 38-year-old employee at a massage parlor. She was married but separated at the time and lived with her elderly mother who in turn, looked after her daughter whilst she was at work.

The scene was set for Somkid. He walked into the parlor requesting a massage; took his time to choose Porntawan and immediately struck up a relaxing conversation while she conducted her massage on him.

Her friends would later talk of how they seemed to get on very well, laughing and flirting together. To them and, just as before, nothing seemed out of the ordinary with this charismatic man.

Porntawan excitedly told her friends of her new client who apparently worked at the very prestigious GPS firm in Bangkok an, that he was seeking an escort for a couple of days to accompany him. She decided to go along with him, and they booked into the Dusit Princess Hotel together.

The following morning, the couple travelled over 135 kms to where they checked into the Piya Mansion Hotel for the evening, located in the Muang District.

But tragically the pattern of his murderous intent was again to be discovered on the 19th June by a cleaning maid who entered their hotel room just around noon.

She was met by what seemed to be a person wrapped in a blanket; there was no movement from the sleeping body and even the air conditioning was on. The maid tried to gently wake the person from their slumber, but she realized that the body was colder than ice and had been gruesomely murdered.

This time when police arrived at the scene, they were overwhelmed with the array of evidence left at the crime scene. Evidence of his brutal murder lay strewn around the hotel room. Uncovering her body from under the blanket, police noticed the severe bruising to Porntawan's neck and, as like his previous victims, she was stripped naked.

Forensics were able to discover that Porntawan had been drugged with anti-allergic tablets which, mixed with alcohol, made for a strong tranquilizer, easily putting Somkid's victim out cold. The potent mixture was discovered in the beer glass that was left in the hotel room along with both Porntawan and Somkid's fingerprints.

Somkid was indeed, mocking his pursuers and would seek out his next victim quickly and precisely.

His 5th victim was Sompong Pimpronpirom, a 36-year-old masseuse and sex worker.

Unfortunately, Sompong met her tragic demise at the hands of Somkid in his usual now characteristic style on 20th June in Buriram, just a few dayss after his last murder.

Again, the couple had been seen checking into a hotel together where Somkid had quickly and callously got to work stripping her naked and strangling her to death. He again, fled the scene taking Sompong's personal belongings, including the cash she was carrying on her.

For the first time, Somkid felt the slight pang of fear creep over him as he realized just how close he was to being caught. Everyone was out to find him and he soon knew that his public lifestyle of staying in upmarket and lavish hotels was over for him.

He had to play it safe. He had to calm down and lie low for a while.

His blatant violent outbursts and incessant lust for murder had been extinguished, just for a short while.

Unbeknownst to the police, baffled as to his whereabouts, Somkid had another secret.

In all his portrayals of a rich charismatic gentleman, Somkid had in fact been leading a double life.

His other quieter persona saw him living in a small unassuming place with his long-time girlfriend and her young son. His hidden family.

Somkid's girlfriend, Kesineewan Pianchayaphum revealed later in both public and police interviews, that she had no knowledge of any murders and did not assist Somkid in any way. She was to speak very fondly of him, stating how she thought he was forced to do extensive travelling for his work, and so, was often away often from home for long periods of time.

Somkid provided for her and her son financially and if truth be told, she had felt extremely safe with him and loved having him around the home.

Kesineewan described him as a quiet gentle man, with good manners who never once raised his voice to them or indeed, never succumbed to any violent tendencies directed toward her or her son. In fact, quite the opposite.

Kesineewan recalled a time when they were sitting together one evening shortly after what was to be, his final murder, watching the news. She recalls laughing with him as the pair watched the breaking news alert featuring a mug shot of a dangerous serial killer that looked just like him.

Thanks to tip offs from Kesineewan's worried neighbors, who identified Somkid as the serial killer, police were soon surrounding his small home. Led by Police Colonel Chadchai Liamsanguan of the Royal Thai Police, the house was quickly secured by heavily armed forces and Somkid arrested and taken in for interrogation.

At the time, leading investigators still remained unclear as to how many victims Somkid actually had under his belt as a number of unsolved cases bearing similarities to his modus operandi, still remained open.

After the investigation held in Bangkok, Somkid admitted to murdering four of the five current cases against him, but refused to admit his involvement in the murder of his fourth victim, Porntawan Pungkhabut. He told police that he had killed the women as they had complained he had not paid them adequately for their services. Somkid was taken to the various crime scenes and asked to reenact how he had taken the lives of his victims. Using a female police officer to visually demonstrate his devious murders, Somkid showed police how he had laid the trap for his unsuspecting victims.

Somkid took immense pleasure and excitement in these reenactment procedures, beaming with pride as he showcased his great performances in the hotel rooms and hotel bathrooms where he took the lives of such innocent and naïve women.

He clearly enjoyed the acts of hunting his prey and savored every second of their agonizingly slow deaths.

Somkid was sentenced to life in prison in late 2005 for one of his murders and, given the death penalty for the other four cases against him.

Somkid's life sentence had started and he would never be able to harm another woman again. All he had to look forward to was his execution date. But by August 2012 his lawyers managed to downgrade Somkid's sentence to life imprisonment only.

He would not hang for his crimes.

If things were not bad enough for the families destroy through Somkid's macabre acts, another atomic shock was to hit them in 2019. After only serving fourteen years of his life sentence, Somkid was given a Royal Pardon effectively presenting him an immediate release for his time already served in prison.

According to official Corrections Facility documents and Department Chief, Navat Savettanan, Somkid had demonstrated such good behavior during his incarceration, becoming a model inmate for all to see.

Unfortunately, and although all Royal Pardons are signed by the now 67-year-old Majesty, King Maha VajraLongkorn, they are done so in bulk and without specificity.

Usually a symbolic gesture in name only, and given out on masse on occasions such as the Kings Birthday, Somkid would now take the pleasure of freedom along with his royal pardon.

Such a distasteful act, it beggars belief how the corrections department did not step in to rectify the matter despite being fully aware of just how dangerous this man had been on the outside world. Releasing a malicious and maniacal murderer who thrived within his carefully constructed narcissistic psychopathy, seemed not to phase the prison nor for that matter, Somkid.

Showing utter and distasteful disregard for the loved ones of those murdered by this sadistic serial killer, the legal system of the country now proffered its leniency to a man who remained without remorse for his evil deeds.

Somkid was now a free man.

Rasamee Mulichand was a 51-year-old single mother of two who worked as a Hotel maid in Khon Kaen and was part of a very close-knit family. Her daughter still lived with her mother at home while Rasamee's son was away studying.

Unknown to her family at the time, Rasamee had started to date online and chatted quit often with men on Facebook. Now divorced, she was looking for a new relationship and, according to her son, Jakkrit Chueakprom, his mother had told him that she had in fact met a very nice man recently on the social media site who was a lawyer and travelled often for his work.

Wanting his mother to be happy once again, Rasamee's son was pleased for her although he did feel that the budding relationship was happening rather too quickly after the suitor had asked to move in with Rasamee, offering to buy her a car and after the pair had been an item for only a few months.

But nonetheless, Rasamee's new partner moved into the family home in early December 2019.

Rasamee had been very excited, telling her daughter and neighbors that they were to be married on the 15th of December. Everyone was extremely happy for her as she waited for her exciting new life to begin as a married woman.

On the morning of 15th December, Rasamee s neighbors had heard an uncomfortable disturbance next door; some type of loud argument and a woman crying out for help. A concerned neighbor quickly knocked on the front door to make sure all was well and was greeted by Rasamee's fiancé whose only reply was that there was no problem at the home.

Sadly, and tragically, Rasamee was found in her home on Sunday evening. She had been brutally murdered, and her soon-to-be fiance had also mysteriously disappeared along with Rasamee's motorcycle. Rasamee's body had been discovered by concerned neighbors who now were left reeling from the ghastly crime scene. It was a scene from a sick vile horror film - her body was placed on her bed; her mouth was taped closed, to stop her screams. Her ankles and wrists were bound with electrical cable and her own mobile charger cable had been found tied so tightly and deeply around her throat that one could almost see the hatred within the murderer's dark soul, screaming out from its tension.

Police Colonel khajornrit Wongrat immediately started investigating the gruesome murder, gathering as much information from the family and neighbors. The Colonel was very much interested in identifying and tracing the whereabouts of the missing boyfriend. Khajornrit searched through Rasamee's social media chat history and recent Facebook posts.

His blood ran cold when he discovered the identity of Rasamee's lover. Staring back at him from the glinting PC screen was the picture of an old acquaintance; it was clearly Somkid pumpuang.

An immediate manhunt was underway for the depraved serial killer and as before, his mugshot was plastered over media outlets and newspapers, but this time offering a large reward to anyone who could help police identify his whereabouts.

The whole country was in shock and maddened that this psycho had been even been released in the first place.

Somkid had killed again, just months after being released in May 2019. His depraved appetite for death had been resurrected only seven months after his Royal Pardon.

Authorities were totally humiliated as a result of their ridiculous blunder.

Informing the public to be on the lookout for the perpetrator, police also drew attention to the distinct scar that Somkid had above his left eyebrow. Very quickly concerned citizens were calling police on the possible whereabouts of the killer who had expertly disappeared once again, as he had done so in the past.

Whilst traveling together on a train from Korat to Bangkok, two students sat chatting together in a packed carriage to pass the time. The female student inadvertently remarked to her friend that the man who was sitting opposite them bared an uncanny resemblance to the wanted serial killer and who the media had now renamed the Thai Jack the Ripper.

The man that was slumped in the seat asleep opposite them, was casually dressed and seemed relaxed. Managing to secretly and quickly capture two photos of the person opposite them using their mobile phone, the students then quietly made their way to a safer area, and posted the pictures to the police website that had been dedicated to finding Somkid.

It took just two calls between the students and local police who informed the petrified students to remain calm and not to arouse any suspicion. At the next available station stop the Thai Royal Police surrounded the train station and stormed the carriage where they suspected Somkid had been seated. Despite wearing a cap and surgical face mask to help disguise his identity, Somkid was quickly restrained and removed from the train by a flurry of uniformed and plain clothed policemen. The public who had been caught up in the turmoil were shocked and started to shout abuse at Somkid who was quickly whisked away by five officers escorting him from the scene.

Searching through his belongings which remained on the train carriage, police discovered that Somkid had armed himself with a large knife. Director Colonel Navat Savettanan later remarked how tragic a mistake it was to have released Somkid given his vicious demeanor and murderous tendencies. He laid the blame squarely at the feet of the Corrections Board but also conceded that often such cases fell through the cracks given that the Thai prison population was often three times over the recommended capacity limits. Excessive overcrowding was the unfortunate norm with most inmates serving time for drug convictions rather than murder.

Somkid was to be immediately interrogated by Thai Pol Colonel Khajornit Wongrat, who asked the Royal courts of Khon Kaen for an immediate extension in order to correctly and thoroughly put together his case.

News Reporters and angry citizens gathered outside the court house and police station where Somkid was being held, hoping to catch a glimpse of this hateful man.

During his testimony, Somkid retraced his footsteps after his recent murder explaining how he escaped the home through an open back window and made his way to a local hospital, where he had already placed Rasamee's motorbike for his planned escape. He would take police investigators to seven local destinations in all before he had finally boarded the train in which he was arrested.

Somkid did however claim that this last murder was in no way premeditated. He told Police in a statement that on the fateful Sunday morning, Rasamee had in fact assaulted him, scratching his face and biting his fingers during an unprovoked argument. It was Rasamee's actions that had caused him to lose control and take her life.

Somkid's narcissism had made him truly believe that the whole incident was the victim's fault. Her actions had caused him to strangle her to death during a fight over car loan payments – the car he had promised to buy her.

At the time of the investigation into Rasamee's death, police had not only discovered the physical evidence of Somkid's fingerprints all over her clothes and blood-stained face which had been so brutally pummelled, but also his personal documentation and a very interesting cell phone device belonging to Somkid's then, secret girlfriend, Sumalee. During her interview with police, Sumalee claimed her ignorance into Somkid's true identity, stating that they ran a noodle shop together and his job was as a travelling lawyer. Sumalee did not even know his real name.

Somkid now stands on trial accused of murder; concealing a body and, theft.

The whole world must now await the much-anticipated murder trial that will no doubt take place this year.

And, while we wait for the court's decision, we must indeed never forget his victims who fell for his charms and false promises. The painful consequences of naivety coupled with innocent desire to better oneself, led to the death of six woman who had sought a way out of the troubled and difficult lives they lived.

It is better to have a difficult life than no life at all.

The Texarkana Moonlight Murders

IRIS HULSE

Texarkana has always been an unusual place. On the east, you have Texarkana, Arkansas, a small town by any other measurement, yet home to the largest population in Miller County. To the west lies Texarkana, Texas, located in rural Bowie County and lucky enough to have its very own Wal-Mart. Together these twin cities make up what is simply referred to as "Texarkana."

Texarkana is a dusty town, built on a foundation of competing railroads and a Mexican border dispute in the 1800s. The town laid low for the next several years, sending off its sons to fight World War I and then II, and welcoming them back home for better or for worse. But no one in Texarkana was prepared for the national attention that came in the spring of 1946. On February 22nd, 1946, a masked serial killer, dubbed the "Phantom Killer" by the *Texarkana Gazette*'s Calvin Sutton, began terrorizing young couples on the town's secluded country roads.

Today, if you search the Internet for information on Texarkana and its morbid history, you will likely be redirected to pages on *The Town That Dreaded Sundown* and its Arkansan producer, Charles B. Pierce. In 1977, decades after the last murders, this film joined the ranks of *Halloween* and *The Texas Chainsaw Massacre* as one of Hollywood's classic horrors, featuring countless local residents as set extras. While the film's accuracy is something to be questioned, it remains a key piece of the town's identity. Visitors can even catch a screening every Halloween at Spring Lake Park, not far from where one of the infamous murders took place.

Texarkana may have embraced its celebrity status, but eighty years ago the town was paralyzed in fear. Within a single spring, five were dead and three were wounded. All in what had previously been a quiet, friendly community.

A Masked Attacker

Just before midnight, on February 22nd, 1946, Jimmy Hollis and Mary Jeanne Larey were finishing up their date in the backseat of

Hollis' father's car. Hollis, 24, and Larey, 19, had been dating for a while, but his parents expected the car (and the lovebirds) home by midnight. Throwing caution to the wind, they parked on a secluded dirt road, known as a lovers' lane, and proceeded to do what young couples will do.

The pair was soon startled by a flashlight, shining through the driver side window and blinding them to whoever stood outside. Hollis quickly composed himself and opened the door, thinking they were being interrupted by an ill-timed police patrol or a prank from some local kids, but they found themselves face-to-face with a masked man holding a gun.

Hollis continued to confront the intruder, telling him, "Fellow, you've got me mixed up with someone else. You got the wrong man." Hollis later said that the masked man muttered something like, "I don't want to kill you, so do what I say." Hollis attempted to calm the assailant, who forced the young man out of the vehicle and demanded Hollis remove his pants, gun pointed squarely at his face. Larey pleaded with Hollis to do as the man said, thinking he would not become violent if they did as he said. Instead the masked man overpowered Hollis, beating him over the head with the revolver. As Hollis lay limp on the cold ground, the attack continued until the sound of Hollis' skull cracking echoed throughout the clearing.

At this point Larey was hysterical with panic, thinking the loud crack of Hollis' broken skull was the sound of him being shot. She told the man they had no money or valuables, attempting to hand the man Hollis' wallet, but he only screamed, "Liar," at her and demanded her purse. Then the masked man told her to run toward the road. Larey ran as fast as she could, but the strange man pursued, continuing to scream, "Liar," at her as she ran.

The assailant eventually outpaced Larey, and forced her to the ground. Larey reported that the man did not rape her, but that assaulted her violent and used his gun to sexually molest her. Larey was afraid for her life, fighting against the weight of her attacker. She eventually managed to escape his grasp, rising up and telling him, "Go ahead and kill me." She then ran to a nearby house at 805 Blanton Street, where she managed to wake up the sleeping woners and pleaded for help. Shortly after, the Bowie County Sheriff, W.H. "Bill" Presley, arrived at what would be the first known Phantom Killer crime scene.

Hollis and Larey were lucky enough to survive this first attack, though they were left with plenty of physical and emotional scars to show for it. Hollis and Larey described their attacker as a tall man wearing a burlap sack with two slits cut for the eyes, though they could not agree on the man's race. Hollis believed the man was white, with tanned skin from working outdoors, while Larey insisted he was a black man because of his mannerisms and "curses." At this point, the attack was treated as a random attempted robbery, it was unknown the chaos that the Phantom Killer would bring in coming months.

The First Kill

In the early hours of March 24th, a truck driver spotted a young man asleep in an Oldsmobile parked on the side of the road. Concerned about the danger of passing traffic, the truck driver ran up to the window, hoping to wake the man and advise him of a better resting area. To the truck driver's horror, the young man was not asleep; he had been shot twice in the back of the head and sat dead in the driver's seat. In the Oldsmobile's backseat was a teenage girl wrapped in a bloody blanket, her body was completely lifeless. These young lovers were not as lucky as the Phantom Killer's first victims.

Richard Griffin, 29, was a retired Navy SeaBee on a double date with his girlfriend of six weeks, Polly Ann Moore, 17, when they pulled over on the highway to have some time alone. They had just finished up dinner with Griffin's sister and her boyfriend at a local café, and Griffin was in no rush to return his girlfriend to her parents' house. Unfortunately, they would never make it home.

Sometime that previous night, Griffin and Moore had pulled over onto the side of the road. It is believed they were approached similarly to the Phantom Killer's first victims, with a blinding flashlight and pointed gun. There was a heavy rainfall over Texarkana that night, so no one would have been out and about to see the killings take place.

Griffin was likely killed first, with two shots from a .32 Colt revolver to the back of his head. Moore, however, had been dragged from the vehicle and sexually assaulted on the cold, wet ground by their attacker. Blood and marks littered the dirt next to the vehicle. After this horror, Moore was also shot and killed by the Phantom Killer. The assailant pulled a blanket from the car's trunk and wrapped her in it before placing her body in the backseat of the Oldsmobile. Any fingerprints and footprints left behind by the killer that night was washed away by the storm.

Griffin's pockets were found empty and turned inside out, and Moore's purse remained at the scene but was emptied of any cash. With the only apparent motive being robbery, questions still remained as to why the crime was carried out so violently. The *Texarkana Gazette*, at the insistence of the Sheriff Bill Presley, made an announcement on March 27th asking residents to not spread rumors or anything else that they did not see with their own two eyes. Despite offering a cash reward, no solid tips ever made it to the police force.

Murder in the Park

Betty Jo Booker, 15, was a straight-A student who was adored by those around her. She worked with Jerry Atkins playing saxophone for a local band, The Rhythmaires, every Saturday night at the local VFW club. On April 14th, she and Atkins, as well as the rest of their band mates, were playing one of their normal shows. Every other weekend, Atkins gave Booker a ride home alternating with a band mate named Ernie Holcomb. This night was Holcomb's night to drive her home, but Booker told Holcomb not to bother because she had a ride set up with an old classmate who was visiting, Paul Martin. Atkins never knew of this change of plans, and until he received a call the next morning he assumed Booker had left with Holcombe, as usual.

Martin's 1946 Ford Coupe was found at 6:30 the next morning by the Weaver family, who were on their way through Texarkana to Prescott, Arkansas. The keys were found still in the car's ignition. Several miles away, in Spring Lake Park, their bodies would be found. Neither the car nor their bodies were anywhere near their destination that night.

Band and classmates claimed that the two were never close to being a couple, and that Booker felt obligated to go out with Martin because of their connection at school. However, no one knows what they were doing pulled over that night, or why they were in that area of town in the first place. No matter what the true story was that night, Booker and Martin would be the Phantom Killer's third and fourth victims.

Like the previous attack, both victims were shot and killed with a .32 Colt semi-automatic revolver. And like the female targets before her, Booker had been sexually assaulted before her murder. After news of the murder was released, hundreds of Texarkana residents flooded the park, hoping to catch a glimpse of the crime scene or help the investigation.

Martin's body was found almost a mile and a half from the abandoned car. He had been shot four times and the ground surrounding his body was covered in his blood.

Booker's body would not be found until five hours later, over three miles from where the car had been found. Booker was found by the Boyd family and Ted Schoeppey, who had joined the community search party to help find the two teenage victims. Booker had been shot twice, and was found with her hand in her coat pocket.

Both bodies showed signs of a struggle against their attacker, yet their fight was unsuccessful. There was no conclusive evidence as to why their bodies were so far from their car.

Booker's missing saxophone played in the running theory of robbery as a primary motive. The police had alerts al over the area, asking people to keep an eye out for a pawned or for sale saxophone matching the serial number of Booker's, and for several months it was considered one of the best leads the authorities had on finding the

killer. Unfortunately for the police, on October 24th, six months after Booker's murder, P. V. Ward and J. F. McNief found the saxophone still in its leather case, just yards from where Booker's body had been found. Ward claimed to know what it was as soon as they stumbled upon it. By the time the case and instrument were turned over to the police, the case had already been labeled closed.

A Red Herring

Public panic over the Phantom Killer was at its all-time high when Virgil and Katie Starks were attacked in their modest farmhouse just ten miles out of town. However, questions would eventually emerge over whether this was truly the work of the Phantom Killer, or if someone else was responsible for the crime.

On the quiet night of May 3[rd,] Virgil, 36, was reading the Texarkana Gazette when two gunshots burst through the front window of their ranch-style home. These bullets hit Virgil in the head, killing him instantly. Katie was lying in bed, already dressed in her nightgown, when she heard the sound of breaking glass. She headed for the living room, where her husband had been seated, only to find him slumped in his armchair, dead. She cried in fear as she reached for the phone, but the attacker shot through her lower jaw, spraying teeth fragments across the Starks kitchen.

In a state of panic and extreme pain, Katie managed to get back up to her feet. She attempted to grab her husband's gun, but was disoriented from being shot. Despite her injuries, she escaped from the house and ran for her sister's down the street. Finding the house empty, she continued to her neighbors' until she found refuge in the Prater house, where the police were finally called. When A. V. Prater answered the door, Katie simply said, "Virgil's dead," before collapsing on the ground. In the time it took for the police to arrive the killer had fled, taking no valuables or anything else of note with him.

Initially, this attack was labeled as another of the Phantom Killer's. It followed the same time pattern as his previous attacks, used a gun as the primary weapon, and targeted a couple. One of the biggest pieces of evidence connecting this attack to the Phantom Killer was a set of unfamiliar tire tracks that matched those found at the other crime scenes. Because of these similarities, many citizens of Texarkana insist that this murder and attempted assault was the Phantom Killer's final blow to the small town's community.

In November 1948, the local authorities made a different conclusion. Another man was arrested and charged with the home invasion and attack on Virgil and Katie Starks. Law enforcement referenced several reasons as to this not being the work of the Phantom Killer, including the fact that the weapon used was a .22 rifle. This change in weapon, as well as the fact this was a home invasion earlier in the evening, pointed police to consider a different suspect entirely.

The town is still home to many skeptics who believe this attack was the Phantom Killer's doing. The crime scene at the Starks home was filled with physical DNA evidence, but at the time DNA testing was only beginning to emerge in the most developed areas of the nation. A little town like Texarkana was nowhere near equipped to handle a case like this, and the DNA evidence was discarded or improperly stored for later testing. While the official stance is that the Phantom Killer was not involved in this attack, the question still haunts many in the area.

A Town In Panic

As the attacks added up, tension in the town of Texarkana grew. After the first and second attack, police forces from both states increased patrols on the town's secluded back roads. A community that had once been friendly, where front doors were never locked and neighbors were always welcome, now grew eerily quiet after sundown.

Businesses saw a decline in customers, especially those catering to the night crowd. Residents were afraid to leave home, even during the daylight, for fear they may become the next target of the Phantom Killer. However, one industry in town became a hotspot for concerned citizens – the local hardware and ammo shops.

Residents bought up guns and ammo like crazy, hoping to be able to defend themselves from the attacks. Deadbolts and other home security devices became commonplace in all the towns households, and some homeowners were even seen setting up booby traps and other contraptions to catch the killer in his tracks.

Many of the town's local high school and college boys rounded up patrol groups. These men would go out at night with baseball bats and other makeshift weapons, hoping to catch the Phantom Killer on the prowl. None of them were ever successful.

Rumors continued to spread and impair the investigations. There was constant news about someone's son being arrested for the murders, or a suspect being charged, but these rumors rarely ever revealed themselves to be true. Police were forced to perform damage control on the stories spreading around town while also conducting their own investigation into the attacks.

Under the Spotlight

After the final attack, at the Starks farmhouse, authorities and media swarmed into Texarkana like never before. The quiet town was buzzing with news reporters from all across the nation, and reports of the murders were spreading to all areas of the country. Texarkana had never experienced the media's curious eye before.

The famous Texas Rangers stepped into the investigation, headed by the well-known Manuel "Lone Wolf" Gonzaullas. Gonzaullas was the first Ranger captain from Spanish descent, and was known for being a ruthless charmer in his day. He spent a great of his time providing interviews for national newspapers and radio broadcasts about the state of the investigation. He was even found one day taking pictures of the Starks crime scene with a young *Life* magazine reporter; neighbors had reported suspicious lights and sounds from the house when Gonzaullas and the woman were found.

While the local press, headed by the Texarkana Gazette, dubbed the suspected serial killer the "Phantom Killer" or "Phantom Slayer," national media clung to a different name: "The Moonlight Murderer." Because of this title, many believe that the murders were all committed under the full moon, when the nights were in fact at their darkest during the time of the crimes.

A Fruitless Investigation

The entire nation was on the lookout for a masked killer terrorizing young couples, with leads coming in from all areas of the South. In all, the authorities considered over four hundred separate suspects, but no one was ever charged with the attacks of that spring. While most of these suspects never received any public attention, the media caught wind of some of the more notable ones.

A middle-aged man from College Station, a Texas town several miles west of Texarkana, was at one point considered a prime suspect. He had previously been caught sneaking up on parked cars, typically with young couples inside, and brandishing a .22 rifle in order to threaten and rob them. While this man was never convicted of murder, many believed him to be the Phantom Killer based on the similar crime and weapon.

In Fayetteville, a young male graduate student of the University of Arkansas committed suicide. In the wake of his untimely death, a note was found containing a handwritten poem and confession to the murders in Texarkana. His military records showed he had showed "homosexual tendencies" during his time with the U.S. Navy, and at the time these tendencies were believed to be a mental disorder related to sexual crimes like rape or assault. Nothing of value ever came from this lead.

Several local residents accused an IRS agent of the crimes, seemingly because of his antisocial demeanor or because he had gotten on the town's bad side. Another man claimed to have committed the crimes during fits of amnesia. Neither of these claims resulted in an arrest.

In 1999 and 2000, several years after the last murder, an anonymous woman called surviving family members of the Phantom Killer's victims, claiming to be his daughter. She apologized for the actions of his crimes and begged for forgiveness from the families. There is speculation over whether these claims are valid, but many believe them to simply be a cry for attention. After all, the primary suspect of the Phantom Killer murders, Youell Swinney, never had a daughter.

Chasing a Criminal

During his time investigating the Moonlight Murders, Max Tackett, an Arkansas law officer, made a puzzling connection. Before each murder a car had been reported stolen and subsequently abandoned on the side of the rode. This information led police to believe that the Phantom Killer was using stolen vehicles to flee the crime scenes, and then dumping them before disappearing into the night.

The next car reported stolen triggered a police stakeout, with law enforcement hoping to find the killer connected to the vehicle. As police closed in on the stolen vehicle, Peggy Swinney was found to be driving. Police seized the car and took Peggy into custody, where she was questioned on how she came to possess the stolen vehicle.

Peggy revealed that Youell Swinney, a known car thief in Texarkana, had given the car to her, but that wasn't all she had to say. Peggy began telling police how Youell was the Phantom Killer, how he had assaulted and murdered all those couples, and how he had made her promise not to tell anyone. She included details of the crimes that had not been given to the public, information only known by police and the killer himself.

Before the police could move in on Youell Swinney, Peggy's story changed. She claimed that her previous confession was a lie, and that Youell was not the Phantom Killer after all. Eventually law enforcement discovered that Peggy and Youell had recently been married, making her unable to testify against her husband at all. While Youell remained an unofficial suspect, it seemed that the police were unable to touch him. But that changed in 1947, when Youell was arrested for auto theft.

At that time, Youell Swinney already had a long criminal record. He had been previously charged with counterfeiting, burglary, and assault, landing him in the Texas State Penitentiary for many years. After his release, he continued his work as a career criminal, but avoided capture for the time being.

During the investigation, police found evidence that Youell had owned a .32 Colt revolver, the murder weapon used to kill the second and third sets of victims, but that he had recently lost the gun in a failed card game. In hi home was also a shirt with the name "Stark" embroidered on the pocket, but it is unknown whether this shirt was actually connected to the Starks murder in the previous year.

With Youell in custody for auto theft, the police attempted to pin him as Texarkana's Phantom Killer. The man had a history of violence and sexual assault, and the record of stolen cars pointed toward his involvement in the murders. Youell never denied his innocence; he simply stayed quiet and refused to work with the police when questioned. A botched injection of "truth serum" during an interview in Little Rock, Arkansas, would eventually end the authorities' questioning of Youell regarding the Moonlight Murders. He was placed in prison for auto theft.

Youell remained in prison until 1973. Many of his cellmates recounted stories that Youell had told them, ones that included intimate details of the Phantom Killer's murder scenes and heavily suggested that Youell knew more than he let on. In 1994, Youell died a free man, never admitting to the Texarkana murders. To this day, most consider Swinney to be the Phantom Killer, even if he never served time for these crimes.

The Missing Woman

On June 1st, 1948, 21-year-old Virginia Carpenter departed Texarkana by train, on her way to her first semester of studying at the Texas State College for Women. She left Union Station at about 3PM, and headed for Denton, Texas and her new life as an educated woman. On the train ride, she met another student by the name of Marjorie Webster, who she shared a taxi with on the way to their dormitories.

Their taxi driver, Edgar Ray "Jack" Zachary, first dropped off Webster at the Fitzgerald dormitories, and then continued on to Brackenridge Hall, where Carpenter would be staying for the term. Zachary reported seeing Carpenter approach two young men in a yellow convertible outside the dorm, saying that she seemed to recognize them and was excited to see them. The next day, Zachary returned to the dorms to deliver some of Carpenter's luggage that she had forgotten at the station. He placed the trunk at the hall's front entrance and left, but no one ever claimed the luggage. That previous night would be the last time Virginia Carpenter was seen.

On June 4th, Carpenter's boyfriend, Kenny Branham, and her mother reported Virginia missing. After being brushed off by authorities, Mrs. Carpenter and other family members left for Denton late in the evening, hoping to help the police find Virginia.

Within several days, there were airplanes, motorboats, and on-foot search parties scanning the surrounding area for any sign of Virginia. Drivers of yellow convertibles were stopped and questioned, and Zachary was questioned by police and subjected to a polygraph test. Carpenter quickly became one of the most famous missing person cases in Texas, with her picture circulating across the country.

Before long, rumors started spreading back in Texarkana. Virginia Carpenter had personally known three of the Phantom Killer's victims, and some started to believe that she had a target on her back. Perhaps the killer had followed her from Texarkana to Denton, just another passenger on the crowded train. Or perhaps the killer was someone that Carpenter knew, like one of the men seen in the yellow convertible to night she went missing. Either way, many believe that this disappearance was connected to the attacks in 1946.

Countless sightings of Carpenter across Texas - riding in a car, buying groceries, or hitchhiking - continued to flow in, but no solid leads were ever discovered. By 1955, Carpenter was considered dead. She had been missing for seven years, and little hope remained of finding her. Despite this, tips continued to emerge on Carpenter's possible whereabouts.

In 1959, a wooden box was found buried with female remains inside that matched Carpenter's physical description. They were sent to Austin for examination, but the landowners soon confessed to digging them up from an old cemetery.

In 1998, a man called the police claiming to know where Carpenter's body was buried. He led police to the grounds of the Texas State College for Women, the school she was meant to attend, but the search came up empty.

Carpenter's disappearance causes some to doubt Youell Swinney's guilt. If her disappearance was a result of the Phantom Killer, the same man who brutally attacked at least three different couples, then this man could not be Swinney. At the time Carpenter went missing, Swinney was being held in prison for auto theft. Maybe Peggy Swinney had a hand in the disappearance of Carpenter, or her abduction was committed by someone other than the Phantom Killer, but it could not have been Swinney.

Phantoms Around the World

Some believe that the Phantom Killer simply moved his crimes to a new location, but it is likely he just inspired other killers to follow his pattern of attack. As the United States reached the height of violent crime and serial killers, attacks cropped up across the country and even abroad. The Phantom Kiiler's *modus operandi* (or M.O.) would become commonplace among serial killers in the coming decades, including the Zodiac Killer, Il Mostro, and the Son of Sam.

In 1946, a young couple was shot in Fort Lauderdale, Florida. Elaine Eldridge and Lawrence Hogan were parked outside Dania Beach when someone approached the vehicle and shot both victims with a .32 semi-automatic handgun. While the weapon used was not a Colt, it remained very similar to the one used in Texarkana. No fingerprints or footprints were found at the scene. With several similarities to the Texarkana attacks, many believed that the killer had relocated across the country. Texas, Arkansas, and Florida police worked together on the investigation, but no major connections were ever revealed to the public.

Located in San Francisco, the Zodiac Killer operated very similarly to the Phantom Killer during the late 1960s. He stalked young people in their vehicles and shot them with a revolver, and his identity remains unknown. However, unlike the Phantom Killer who personally avoided the media's attention, the Zodiac Killer was hungry for exposure. His main source of fame comes from sending cryptic notes to the Bay Area press, including four ciphers. Only one of these ciphers was ever solved, but it led the police no closer to identifying a suspect. These notes were examined top to bottom, in hopes of finding the true identity of the Zodiac Killer, but no leads were ever found.

Across the Atlantic Ocean, from 1968 to 1985, Florence, Italy was shook by sixteen murders. Dubbed Il Mostro or The Monster of Florence, the killer shot young couples parked alone in their cars with a .22 rifle. While four different suspects were arrested and charged with these murders throughout the years, the investigation has attracted scrutiny and many believe these men were actually innocent.

While the Son of Sam's identity is known today, his killings reflected those of the Phantom Killer and others. Operating in New York City in the mid 1970s, David Berkowitz killed six victims with a .44 Bulldog revolver. His attacks triggered the biggest manhunt in New York City, and for years women kept their hair short and avoided disco clubs for fear of being Berkowitz's next target. Like the Zodiac Killer, Berkowitz loved taunting the police and media with cryptic letters, where he promised to continue killing until he was caught. After his capture in 1977, Berkowitz enjoyed a bit of morbid celebrity for his crimes, which many reported he seemed to enjoy greatly. He remains in prison today, serving six life sentences.

While it is unlikely that the Phantom Killer actually relocated to be the Zodiac Killer or Il Mostro, some true crime experts believe it is possible. While the Phantom Killer was one of the first of his kind, looking back his killings were not exceptionally unique by today's standards.

It is easy to see how the Phantom Killer and his Moonlight Murders have shaped our ideas of killers today. Urban legends of a mad man stalking young couples in love, scratching on car doors and leaving bloody hooks behind, persist around campfires and in dark corners of the Internet. *The Town That Dreaded Sundown* might live among the likes of Freddy Krueger and Michael Myers, but it is a fictionalized retelling of the very real horrors that haunted Texarkana that year.

House of Horror : The True Story of Rosemary West

Mary Gilmore

Unfortunately, it's not unusual in this day and time to turn on the news and hear a warning about a new serial killer roaming our streets. It's horrifying and hard to comprehend what could possibly make a person commit such heinous crimes. What is wrong with this person that drives him or her to commit such an act? The truth is that people have searched for the answers to that question for a very long time. Unfortunately, it still remains a mystery for the most part.

Rosemary West is one of those baffling cases. We will look deeper into her life and learn how her inner demons progressed to becoming one of Britain's most notorious and sadistic serial killers, taking the lives of at least 10 young women and girls.

Most of the information obtained by the authorities came from her husband and partner in crime, victims who escaped or were permitted to leave, and a great deal from her own children. Rosemary has offered very limited insight into the story, even to this day.

Remarkably, she did not act alone in committing these grisly deeds. This story is immensely complex, which I will attempt to sort out and then tie it all together with the union of Rose Letts West and Fred West in their vicious killing spree. There will be accounts of child abuse, rape, sexual deviance, torture, and murder. Rosemary West's crimes were so horrendous; it may be difficult for some of you to read.

Rosemary West's Early Life

Rosemary's mother came into her room one morning to wake her for school. Rosemary probably knew by the familiar expression on her mother's face that this would be one of those mornings that fills her life with constant dread. As she gets dressed, she begins preparing herself for what she knows is probably about to occur.

As she walks into the kitchen, breakfast is the last thing on her mind. Instead, she braces herself for the punishment she is about to receive. Don't misunderstand, Rosemary hadn't done anything wrong, but her father didn't need a reason.

His kind of punishment wasn't a time-out or a swat on the behind as most children receive. His were the kind that affect a child for a lifetime. Rose has no idea whether she is about to be beaten or if she'll endure other horrors that her father is known to inflict.

That is a likely scenario in the life of Rosemary West. Her father was a paranoid schizophrenic. The mental illness along with other problems, made life for her, her mother, and her siblings a nightmare. The abuse was bad enough, but what made it even more terrifying was not knowing from one minute to the next when or why her father's rage would erupt.

As a result of her home life, Rose made bad grades and became overweight. To make her situation worse, she was teased and bullied at school, giving her no relief from the continuous damage to her self-esteem.

There's a possibility that Rosemary's destiny was sealed much earlier in her life. It's not surprising that Rosemary's mother suffered from severe depression. The illness was so debilitating that she received electroconvulsive therapy several times while Rosemary was still in the womb, one of which occurred just before Rosemary's birth. There were some that thought this therapy was the reason for Rosemary's frequent outbursts of anger as well as her inability to do well in school.

Most of us would be unable to imagine a childhood such as the one led by Rosemary West.

Why do They Kill?

There are no exact traits of a serial killer to help us understand what drives them to kill. Some of them come from a two parent loving home while others have divorced parents. Some had abusive parents and others had loving parents.

Some think it's due to a head or brain injury sometime in their life; however, most people that have had brain injuries do not become killers. The majority of serial killers are men who act alone. Rosemary is not only a woman, she also had a partner in her life of crimes. Female killers and couples represent only a small percentage of serial killings.

The Federal Bureau of Investigation did a symposium, which was comprised of 135 experts who have dealt with serial killers in various ways to determine commonalities of serial killings. They determined that there are no definitive common traits. However, the central nervous system is constantly developing in adolescence, which determines a person's social coping system. That is, they develop the way they interact with their peers such as in negotiation and compromise. If it does not develop adequately, it can result in violent behavior.

It would be safe to say that the events of Rosemary West's childhood could be a factor in the choices she made later in life.

Rosemary's Life Before the Murders

Rosemary Letts was the fifth child born to Bill and Daisy Letts in Devon, England on the 29th of November in 1953. She normally went by the shorter version of her name, Rose. As we've seen, Rose's childhood was unlike most other children's. In pictures of Rose at a younger age she had an ever present smile on her face. You wouldn't guess that she was going through hell within the walls of her home.

The Letts family lived in Northam, a charming seaside town in Devon. Neighbors thought of Bill Letts as a nice man; however, they must have thought it strange that they rarely saw his children. When they did, the children were mainly seen walking around in their garden. One neighbor stated that they really didn't seem to be playing at all. They were just walking around and rarely seen outside the walls of the garden.

What they didn't know was that the children weren't allowed outside the walls and were afraid to play because they were forbidden to get dirty.

Although Rose's father constantly punished the children including Rose, he was not as physically abusive with Rose as with his wife and the other children. It was thought that he didn't physically abuse her as much as the others because he thought there was something not quite right about her.

Some people thought that he didn't hurt Rose as much because he was using her for his sexual pleasures instead. Others speculated that Rose learned at a very young age that she could control her father's anger by using sex.

Rose's mother Daisy, eventually left her father. She moved out of their house taking Rose and the other children with her, freeing them from the abusive environment. Remarkably, after a brief time, Rose moved back in with her father who resumed sexually abusing her.

One day, as Rose waited for a bus, she was approached by a man. Rose described him as a dirty man who had disgusting green teeth. She and the man struck up a conversation and even though his appearance was repulsive by most people's standards, Rose became attracted to him. The man's name was Fred West.

West was raising his daughter and stepdaughter at that time so Rose began babysitting the two girls. In addition, Rose and Fred also became a couple.

Fred's Early Years

Fred West, the son of Walter and Daisy West, was born in Much Marcle, England in 1941. He was the second of their six children. Growing up, he was considered to be a nice boy. They appeared to be a normal family, however, Fred's upbringing was perhaps even worse than Rosemary's. According to Fred, the motto around his house by his father was, "Do whatever you want, just don't get caught."

Fred would later reveal to police that incest was a common occurrence in his household. He said his father regularly had sex with his own daughters. Fred also claimed that his father introduced him to bestiality. In addition, it was thought that his mother Daisy took his virginity when he was 12-years-old.

Not surprising, Fred did not do well in school and dropped out at the age of 15. Two years later, he was involved in a tragic motorcycle accident. He received a broken arm and leg and a fractured skull. The head injury put him in a coma for eight days. Afterward, his family claimed that thereafter, he frequently become enraged without warning. Amazingly, two years later, he received another head injury. In this instance, he fell from a fire escape causing unconsciousness for 24 hours.

Fred's history of child abuse and head injuries would certainly coincide with the conceivable characteristics of a serial killer.

At the age of 20, he was caught and arrested for molesting a 13-year-old girl who subsequently became pregnant. He was convicted, but for unknown reasons he was not sentenced to prison. The reason is possibly because the girl's parents and Fred's parents were friends. Even with his family's propensity for deviant sexual acts, they had recently decided to try their hand at getting religion, therefore, they disowned Fred after this latest incident.

Fred had problems keeping a normal job. He landed a construction job; however, he was caught stealing. In addition, he continued to get caught molesting more young girls. It's amazing how he could still be roaming the streets even back at that point.

Shortly after, when West was around 21, he ran into a former girlfriend named Catherine Costello. She was better known as Rena, which was the name she used while prostituting and the name stuck. In addition, Rena was an accomplished thief. Nevertheless, even with her reputation, she was described by neighbors and other acquaintances as a very nice person and an exceptionally good mother.

Even though she was already pregnant with another man's child at the time, things heated up between her and Fred again and they married about two months later. The baby girl was born in February

1963 and was named Charmaine. Rena had another child by Fred a year later and named her Anna Marie. You will hear the names of these two girls in a shocking context later in the story.

Unbelievably, someone gave Fred West a job driving an ice cream van. This wouldn't seem a proper job for Fred the child molester to say the least. For Fred, it was the perfect job with young girls running after him. It was an ideal way for him to find victims.

While working at this job, a four-year-old boy ran into the street in front of his van and the child was killed. After this incident, even though the death was accidental, Fred feared people in the area would seek retribution for the boy's death. He thought it would be in his best interest to move away.

At the time, a woman named Isa McNeil was caring for the West's children. Additionally, Rena had become friends with a young woman named Anne McFall. They all moved with Fred to *The Lakeside* caravan park in Bishop's Cleeve, Gloucestershire, which is where Fred would later live with Rose.

With Fred's sadistic habits still intact, there were soon problems in this odd household. Fred insistently pushed his warped sexual necessities onto all three women. It became too much for his wife, Rena, and the children's nanny, McNeil, so the two of them moved to Scotland. On the other hand, the other woman, Ann McFall, had warmed up to Fred and stayed behind. Besides, she had already become impregnated by him.

Fearful of Fred, Rena and Isa's planned was to keep their departure secret from him and sneak away. Unfortunately, McFall told Fred, which enraged him. He allowed them to leave, but not with the two children, so the two women fled to Scotland. Rena returned frequently to visit her children.

After that, McFall began to pressure Fred to divorce Rena and marry her. Apparently, this didn't set well with Fred. When she was eight months pregnant with Fred's child, she completely vanished. She was never reported missing, but her body was later discovered in a field minus her fingers and toes, which had been removed and were missing.

Fred was left to care for his daughter and stepdaughter.

The Evil Duo Unites

Around this time is when Fred met Rose at the bus stop. It was at the time when Fred was caring for his step-daughter and biological daughter, so Fred already had at least the one murder of Anne McFall under his belt when he met Rose. Rose then began taking care of the two children.

When they first got together Rose was only 16-years-old and Fred was 12 years older at 28. Her father absolutely disapproved of the relationship. He threatened West that if he didn't leave Rose alone he would call Social Services due to Rose's young age. That was ironic since her father had been having sex with her himself for a long time. Of course, that was most likely the reason he didn't want her to go.

Nevertheless, Rose moved in with Fred and they lived together as a family with Fred's two daughters. After only about two months, they married she moved in with him at *The Lakeside Caravan Park* in Bishop's Cleeve, Gloucestershire, where Fred had lived with Rena and Anne.

Of course Fred, a man of few scruples, soon introduced his young and damaged wife to a sadistic world of pornography and urged her into prostitution. Due to Rose's demoralizing childhood, it didn't take a lot of urging for her to become caught up in his world.

Not one to hold down a regular job, Fred's contribution to the income was mainly by thievery. He wasn't very accomplished at that either and was frequently caught and arrested. It wasn't long before he was sent to prison for 10 months, leaving young Rose in charge of his two daughters.

To make matters worse, she had become pregnant and gave birth to her daughter, Heather, in 1970 while Fred was still in jail. Being young in addition to having mental problems, caring for three children was a tall order for Rose and she didn't handle the situation well, to say the least.

To add to the pressure, seven-year-old Charmaine, began to be unruly and Rose was unable to cope with it. Years later, according to the other child, Anna Marie, it was not unusual for both girls to receive severe beatings; however, no matter how bad the beating, Charmaine refused to cry. This infuriated Rose so it's no surprise that Charmaine didn't seem to be around any longer after that.

This is thought to be when Rose committed her first murder. Rose's tendency to lose her temper most likely caused her to loss control and kill Charmaine. Apparently, Rose hid the girl's body, because it's known that Fred disposed of the body after he returned from prison.

Fred would hold this over Rose in the future. On one of the occasions when Rose's father tried to convince her to leave Fred and come home, Fred made a remark that was something like, "Come on now Rose, you know what we have between us." For someone that didn't know Fred, it would sound like an expression of love. More than likely with Fred, it was his not so subtle way of saying, "You can't leave. I have too much on you." She later told her parents that Fred would do anything, including murder.

Fred's first undertaking after returning from jail was to dismembered and dispose of Charmaine's body. For whatever sick reason, as with Anne McFall, he removed her fingers and toes and then buried her. This became the normal process in Fred's body disposal. It was later speculated that Fred and Rose were possibly involved in Satan worship. It is thought by some that removing the fingers and toes of their sacrifices was typical for Satan worshipers.

The next time Rena Costello came to visit her daughter it naturally created a problem when she discovered her daughter's absence, thanks to Rose. As you can imagine, Rena was not happy about her missing daughter and demanded some answers. Therefore, Rose and Fred must have decided that Rena would have to go as well. So this visit to see her little girl resulted in Rena's demise as well. Minus her fingers and toes, she was buried in a field close to the Caravan Hotel where Rose and Fred still lived.

That meant a total of at least three people had already lost their lives courtesy of Fred and Rose West. One each for Rose and Fred and now Rena by both of them.

A brief time later, Rose gave birth to their second child, Mae. They bought a large two-story house in Gloucester; however, there was not much money coming in. Fred started putting up panels in the rooms to create multiple bedrooms called bedsits. They were tiny rooms, which didn't fit much more than a bed. They began renting out these rooms for extra income; however, the rooms served another purpose as well.

By this time, Rose's fulltime career had become *prostitute*. They also began working other women out of the house. One of the rooms labeled "Rose's Room" was dedicated to Rose for turning tricks. Outside the door was a red light, which was lit when the room was in business. The children knew they were not to disturb when the red light was on. The room also came complete with a peephole, which was Fred's method for watching his wife in action and for making videos.

Both Rose and Fred had come from a family where incest was normal. It was not unnatural to them when Rose's own father occasionally came to their house to have sex with her.

In around October of 1972, Rose and Fred hired Carol Owens as a new nanny for their children. She told her story years later stating that Fred and Rose attempted to bring her into their twisted lifestyle. Not wanting any part of it, she soon left their house.

A few weeks later, as she was walking home, Fred pulled up beside her and offered a ride. The next thing she knew he hit her on the head. When she awoke, her hands were tied and Fred was in the process of taping her mouth.

She was told that if she tried to resist, Fred would call in his friends and let them have their way with her and she would then be killed.

They said they would bury her under the paving stones outside their home along with hundreds of other girls. Terrified, she didn't attempt to resist.

Unbelievably, they allowed her to leave the next day and she proceeded to file charges on them. Fred somehow managed to convince the court that the sex was consensual. In addition, Owens decided that testifying against these two could be an unhealthy choice.

The couple was given a meager fine on a charge of indecent assault and then released. She would be the last victim that the Wests' would allow to leave alive.

Years later, she regretted not testifying. She felt that if she had, it could have saved the lives of numerous women and girls and she was most likely correct.

One day, Fred and Rose arrived home and their neighbor, Elizabeth Agius, was outside. She had become friendly with the couple, so Fred stopped for a chat. Just in conversation, she asked what they had been doing, so Fred proceeded to tell her exactly what they had been up to.

He said they were cruising around looking for young girls. He must have felt he needed to explain why his wife would go along with him on such an outing. He said they figured the girls would see Rose and wouldn't be scared to get in the car. She would later say that she thought he must be joking...he wasn't.

Meanwhile, Fred was busy redecorating the cellar. One of the prostitutes that worked in the house later told authorities that she saw black suits, masks, chains, and whips down there. Fred had created his own torture chamber.

Anna Marie, Fred's remaining child with Rena Costello, was the first to be brutalized in Fred's torture chamber. She was bound, gagged, and violently raped as Rose watched. She was only eight-years-old at the time and this treatment would continue for years.

Eventually, Anna Marie moved out of the house to live with her boyfriend, which quite possibly saved her life. Again, letting her go would prove to be a bad move for the Wests later in court. As one of the survivors, a considerable amount of the horror stories came from her.

After Anna Marie's departure, Fred's attentions naturally turned to his daughters Heather and Mae; however, Heather wanted no part of it and resisted. Understandably, she was unable to keep it to herself and told a friend about the horrors happening at home. This would seal her fate, but Fred later claimed to police that her death was accidental.

The life of Rose and Fred West continued filled with the unimaginable. They would go on to have a total of seven children who were born in a short time span. It is believed that three are by Fred, one is by her own father, and the remaining three are from her clients. It almost seemed that their reason for having children was so Fred and Rose would have someone to torture at the times when no one else was tied up in the cellar. You can certainly say with certainty that Fred and Rose West were definitely not loving parents.

The One's That Didn't Survive the Terror

Over the next few years, the abuse of the West's children continued as did the murders of others. At some point, Fred went to work at a slaughter house. It was thought that this is when his already violent habits became even more gruesome. It could have been a factor in his fascination for dismembering his victims.

It is believed the next victim was Lynda Gough who was a personal acquaintance of the West's. She enjoyed participating in some of their sexual activities by sharing sex partners with Rose. However, for unknown reasons she later vanished. Gough's mother came to the West's house looking her daughter and was told that she moved in order to pursue a job. While she was speaking to the woman, Rose was wearing some of Linda Gough's clothing.

Carol Ann Cooper, only 15-years-old, is thought to be the next victim. She disappeared while walking home from the movies.

Evidence showed she died by strangulation, was dismembered, and buried in the garden.

Lucy Partington was in town visiting her family and a friend over the Christmas holidays. She went to the bus station to take a bus back home and most likely Fred, being one to hang out at bus stations asked her if she wanted a ride. As Fred and Rose planned, it is thought that the only reason she let them even approached her was due to the presence of Rose.

It is thought that they kept Partington in captivity for about a week after she vanished because poor Fred showed up at the hospital about a week later with a large laceration needing stitches. Authorities think he received the cut while cutting up Partington.

Shirley Hubbard went missing when she was returning home from Droitwich. There was definitive evidence of her torture. Her head was completely wrapped with tape with only a short rubber tube in her mouth to breath.

Juanita Marian Mott was a former tenant of the Wests'. Her torture was obvious. She was gagged with a binding made of socks, tights, and a bra, which were all stuffed inside each other. She was also tied up with clothes line rope looped around her thighs, arms, wrists, and ankles. This was done with the rope going back and forth around her horizontally and vertically until she was completely immobilized. She also had a rope with a noose, which most likely suspended her from the rafters in the cellar.

Shirley Anne Robinson was one of the prostitutes that worked out of their house who had sexual relations with both Fred and Rose. She became pregnant by Fred, at the same time Rose was pregnant by one of her clients.

Shirley began to get the idea she would like to replace Rose, which is not advisable in this family. Rose demanded that she had to go. She and her unborn child were dismembered and buried in the back garden. The cellar was full of bodies by this time and the back garden became the new burial grounds.

Therese Siegenthaler was a hitchhiker in route from London to Ireland. Some of the evidence showed that like Partington, she was kept alive for close to a week during which time she was likely tortured and raped.

Allison Chambers was the last known non-related victim. She was killed in 1979.

Their oldest daughter, Heather Ann West, was the last known victim. Fred claims he killed her by accident. His story of the "accident" went something like this. He told police that Heather was being extremely insolent so he had to slap her. She then started laughing at him so he was forced to grab her by the throat to stop her from laughing. He said that unfortunately, he must have grabbed her too tightly because she began to turn blue and stopped breathing. He tried to revive her by putting her in the tub and running cold water on her, but it didn't work.

He then removed her clothes and attempted to put her in a garbage bin, but she didn't fit. Back into the tub she went so he could make her smaller, but he first strangled her with a cord to make sure she was dead. He told police he didn't want to start cutting her up and then have her come alive on him.

He also closed her eyes before he started cutting. He said he couldn't dismember her while she was looking at him. He must have been hearing a strange sound because he told police he found the source of a noise when he cut off her head. He said it was a horrible and unpleasant sound like scrunching. He also said that after cutting her up, she fit quite nicely into the garbage bin.

She was later put in a hole that the West's son, Stephen, had dug with the intention of it becoming a fishpond. Fred put Heather in the hole and built a patio over it. Stephen had unknowingly dug the grave for his own sister's burial.

Police also believed that they killed 15-year-old Mary Bastholm in 1968, though they never found her body. The Wests' son Stephen, later told authorities that he believes Bastholm was one of his father's earlier murders because his father boasted about it.

The Evidence Begins to Surface

Oddly, they violently murdered many of their victims, but then set others free after they had finished using and abusing them. Naturally, some of them went to the police.

The released victims were some extremely lucky women to say the least. Their reports finally got the attention of a Detective Constable named Hazel Savage. Savage was also familiar with Fred West and his arrests for thievery and child molestation through the years since the time he was married to Rena Costello.

Fred videoed an incident in which he raped Anna Marie while Rose held her arms. Anna Marie told friends about her home life who in turn told their parents. This and other information got back to Savage.

This enabled the Detective to obtain a warrant to search the West's property. It was the beginning of the needed evidence to finally remove these damaged and dangerous monsters from the unsuspecting public.

Fred was arrested and charged with rape and sodomy of a minor and Rose for assisting in the rape of a minor. Amazingly, Fred and Rose West were still not suspected of murder. At this time, the younger children were removed from the home.

Due to the evidence found in the home, Detective Savage had the suspicion that there was more going on here and she began digging deeper into this strange family. She had a feeling that there was something suspicious concerning the whereabouts of their daughter Heather and she was determined to find out.

For instance, it was noticed in the videos of the West's and their children that was seized from their home that Heather was never present. Also, in interviews with some of the children, they said something that should not come from the mouths of children.

Apparently, there was a common joke around the West house. Fred told the children that he would buried them under the patio with their sister Heather if they didn't behave.

Unbelievably, the case fell apart when two of the main witnesses decided not to testify. Detective Savage continued questioning the children repeatedly to no avail. Fred and Rose had programmed them and put enough fear in them by then that they would no longer say anything to help the case.

However, the evidence together with case workers reporting the family joke about their sister Heather kept Detective Savage searching. It also appeared that another child, Charmaine, was missing as well. Eventually, Savage put together enough evidence to obtain a warrant to dig on the Wests' property.

Soon after that, Rose answered the door to find the police with warrant in hand. She quickly called Fred to tell him the police were about to dig on their property and they're looking for Heather. It turned out that Fred would be of little help because it took him four hours to get home. He came up with some excuse about passing out due to inhaling paint fumes at work.

Could it have been that Fred was busy disposing of evidence such as fingers and toes or perhaps he had a burial he had not gotten around to completing. That will never be determined.

They began searching the house in addition to excavating the garden in February 24, 1994. The dig was originally intended to search for the body of the daughter Heather, which they soon found. Fred was brought in by the police for questioning the next day. He surprised the police by confessing to the murder of his daughter Heather and he repeatedly told police that Rose knew nothing about it.

Fred and Rose must have been up all that night getting their stories straight. It is thought that Fred assured Rose he would take all the blame and she shouldn't worry. Fred was good to his word, at least in the beginning.

Meanwhile, after the attending pathologist began inspecting the bones of Heather, he brought it to the attention of the police that there was an extra leg bone indicating the presence of at least one other body.

After that discovery, Fred decided he should do some damage control by telling police the location of Alison Chambers and Shirley Robinson's bodies. He hoped this would prevent them from doing any more digging.

It was first thought that Fred did this to avoid being categorized a serial killer, which is someone that kills more than three people. Unbelievably, as it turned out, Fred wanted the police to stop digging because he didn't want his cherished home to be torn apart any further.

Nevertheless, they continued and began to find more human bones. Rose was not arrested until around March 4, 1994. Even then, it was only for sex offenses. Fred had trouble deciding for sure if he wanted to protect Rose after all. He would go on the recant his confession that he killed Heather and then later changed his mind again saying Rose was innocent.

In Britain, prisoners are sometimes assigned an "appropriate adult", which is someone that assists and basically befriends the prisoner. This was normally done for juveniles; however, Janet Leach was assigned to Fred. Leach didn't know she was about to become the confidant of a serial killer.

It turned out that Fred became comfortable enough with Leach that he soon told her the whole gory story. She pointblank asked him if there were more victims. Fred responded that there were six more and went on to draw a sketch of his house and garden complete with the locations of the graves.

Fred knew exactly where they were located; however, he had some trouble remembering all their names. He recalled one that had a scar on her hand; therefore, Scar Hand became her name. Another he called Tulip because he thought she was Dutch, although she was actually Swiss.

Fred was now on a roll and confessed to the murders of his ex-wife Rena Costello and ex-lover, Anne McFall. He told leach that he dumped them nearby his childhood home. He then confessed that he buried his step-daughter Charmaine, Fred's child that Rose killed, close to the hotel where they lived in Gloucester. Strangely, Fred would admit to the murders, but he would not admit to the rapes.

Meanwhile, Rose continued to play the role of an innocent woman, denying any involvement in the murders. She went so far as to act horrified at the actions of her perverted husband. When Fred attempted to contact her, she snubbed him not wanting to have anything to do with such a despicable person.

After making bail, Rose moved into a halfway house with her son Stephen and her daughter Mae. The police were not convinced of her innocence and bugged the house. Nevertheless, Rose stuck to it and never spoke of anything that would involve her in murder. Only charges of sexual offense remained against her.

As can be imagined, the town of Gloucester was flooded with the media. The attention had a tremendous impact on the small town. The West's house became known by the appropriate name "The House of Horrors". The residents were in disbelief that this unimaginable crime spree had gone on in their town for 20 years.

The Trial

As it turned out, Fred took the easy way out. He hanged himself in his jail cell by tying together bed sheets leaving Rose to deal with the whole state of affairs.

She was finally charged with 10 of the murders since Rena Costello and Anne McFall were before she was on the scene. She went to trial in October of 1995.

One after another, witnesses took the stand and told their shocking stories. One of the highest drama moments of the trial came with the testimony of Fred's oldest daughter, Anna Marie. She was on the stand for two days. At one point she looked her stepmother straight in the eye as she told a story of sexual abuse and torture that began when she was a little girl of only eight-years-old.

She recalled the incident when she was so savagely raped by her father while Rose held her arms. During the incident, Rose was telling her how lucky she was to have parents to show her how to please her husband when she gets married. She said she was hurt so badly that she couldn't attend school for several days. She also recalled a day that her father strapped her down and raped her while he was home for a quick lunch break. These were only two of the many horror stories she lived.

The second day of her testimony was delayed for several hours because she took an overdose of pills the previous evening.

Another person that offered a wealth of damaging testimony was Fred's *Appropriate Adult* and confidant, Janet Leach. However, she became so stressed that she suffered a stroke during the trial causing another delay. It wasn't until later after the trial's end that Leach could tell police the entire story that Fred confided in her.

One of the key witnesses was Carol Owens who was one of the girls they brought home under the pretense of being a nanny. She was allowed to leave, but only after she endured their sadistic sexual torture. Needless to say, she had tales to tell.

Another witness who is still referred to as Miss A was lured to the West house and saw two naked girls who were being held prisoner. She watched as they were tortured and raped. She was then raped by Fred and sexually assaulted by Rose. She was one of the lucky ones that left that cellar with her life.

It wasn't hard for the jury to come back with a unanimous verdict of guilty on 10 counts of murder. Rose received life in prison.

The Aftermath

The "House of Horrors" at 25 Cromwell Street in Gloucester where nine bodies were found was demolished in October of 1996; however, there seemed to be a curse that affected many of the people associated with Rose and Fred West.

John West, Fred's brother, hanged himself while awaiting his trial for the rape of his own niece Anna Marie.

Anna Marie continued to suffer from the memories of her distorted childhood. In 1999, she attempted suicide by jumping from a bridge. She was rescued, leaving her to live another day with the memory of the horrors from her past.

Stephen West, the son of Rose and Fred, attempted to commit suicide in 2002 in the same manner as his father and uncle by hanging himself. However, it wasn't meant to be because the rope broke.

The actual number of murders will remain a mystery. During his interrogation by the police, Fred stated that there were two more bodies buried in shallow graves that they would never find.

He also told them there were 20 other bodies spread around in various places. He claimed he would show the police the location of one body each year. One wonders if he knew at that time that he would later take his own life and wouldn't be following through with that promise.

Fred took any other secrets he had in his evil little mind with him to his grave. After that, Rose wasn't interested in discussing the matter any further.

According to an article in the DailyMail, dated February 2014, even though Rose West filed for a couple of appeals after she went to prison, she has now decided she never wants to leave her top security jail cell at Low Newton jail in Durham and why would she, her cell is equipped with TV, radio, CD player, and private bathroom. She has never confessed to committing any murders.

Authorities know the women and girls were tortured, raped, killed, dismembered, and buried; however, they don't know the details of many of those crimes. Rose has been asked by numerous people to give those details, but she refuses.

Conclusion

This is an account of actual facts; however, it hard to believe that it's anything other than a fictional horror story.

Even after hearing about the disturbing childhoods of both Rose and Fred West, it's difficult to understand the extent of their warped minds. Even more disturbing is the fact that two people that are this broken can find one another and carry out their evil deeds together.

This story brings us no closer to the answer of what drives serial killers. Both Rose and Fred were abused as children mainly by their fathers; however, it was young women and girls that were the focus of their punishment.

There have been books and a movie made about them to show us how this horrific story unfolds. However, only in our minds can we come close to conjuring up the evil that occurred within the walls of 25 Cromwell Street. We may never know the full extent of the terrors that transpired.

The fact that Fred West is gone and Rose West will never see the light of day should make us all sleep a little more soundly.

THOMAS LEE DILLON

JOANNE DILLER

Thomas Lee Dillon's story is not one of the more well-known in the history of serial killers, but it is a convoluted and sometimes bizarre tale that kept people guessing for four years during the late 1980s and early 1990s. Like many serial killers, Dillon's past was not an incredibly unique one, up until the time of his first murder. He was born in July of 1950, and lived in the town of Magnolia in Ohio. He was married, had a son, and worked at the Canton Ohio Waterworks for over a decade of his adult life. Although he was often given to flights of fancy, friends of Dillon's would never have suspected that he was the mastermind behind a series of murders that took place in Ohio over the course of four years.

Some of the people who knew Dillon the best, however, began to notice disturbing patterns in his behavior after his later murders. What might have seemed to be simply an unnecessarily cruel streak eventually became undeniable proof that Dillon was actually a much darker individual than he appeared on the surface. The more he murdered, the more he began to feel an insatiable desire to continue killing. Over time, his violence turned toward animals, and he began to destroy innocent pets in between taking human lives. He started setting fires and imagined himself as some sort of hero as he made his way across the farmlands of Ohio, leaving a trail of destruction in his wake. In fact, Dillon was prone to many different forms of imagination, many of which pitted him as some sort of underdog against a difficult foe, and all of which led to real world violence.

One of Dillon's favorite fantasies involved imagining himself as a special ops soldier, sent on some sort of secret mission to hunt down military targets. The more he thought about this, the more he found himself wanting it to become a reality. One day, the line between his imagination and the real world blurred a little too much, and Dillon became a murderer for the first time. As a part of the same delusional behavior, he would eventually go on to kill four other people, for a grand total of five sniping murders by the time of his eventual arrest.

It was very difficult for police to pinpoint the source of the murders. Over time, Dillon earned a serial killer profile, which described him as someone who actually enjoyed committing crimes and did not perform them out of some sense of obligation alone. The profile also specified that the murderer was a white male with a college education, which described Dillon perfectly. However, it mistakenly pegged him as a man in his late 20s, when in fact he was in his late 30s and early 40s during the times when he committed the murders. The profile was also incorrect in that it believed Dillon to live near all of his victims, when in fact he lived over a hundred miles away from some of them. Because of his many fantasies, he would often get completely lost in his own mind, and drive for hours before he found a victim.

In fact, this quickly became Dillon's preferred method of choosing his victims. He would get into his truck and start cruising down the road, beer in hand, simply thinking. Most of his thoughts began in simple ways, and his ideas might have belonged to anyone. However, it did not take long before his mental delusions began to turn much more dark. As he continued to drive, he would have another beer, and another, and eventually he would hear voices telling him that there were some unpleasant deeds he needed to attend to. It would not be long, then, until he happened upon some unsuspecting person in the middle of Ohio's countryside, and would do exactly what the voices wanted, without any sense of remorse after the fact. This disturbing trend was not apparent in Dillon's initial criminal profile, but eventually came to the surface as more and more of the mystery was untangled.

Perhaps it is Dillon's sense of normalcy that makes him such a frightening player in the history of American serial killers. Despite his terrifying track record, he appeared, at his core, to be a normal man that might have passed by anyone on the street without so much as a second glance. In order to understand the true horror behind Thomas Lee Dillon, however, it is important to look beyond the first chapters of his life and personality, and delve much more deeply into the story behind his murders.

First Murder

Southern Ohio has never been known as a very violent place. Up until Thomas Lee Dillon broke onto the scene in 1989, there had never been so much as an inkling of serial murder in this part of the country. The first of Dillon's murders singlehandedly destroyed the idyllic world of Southern Ohio, however, bringing the very real possibility of serial crime into the world of this quiet part of the United States. Although no one yet knew it at the time, the seemingly random and unprovoked murder of Donald Welling, age 35, actually came about as part of Dillon's delusions of grandeur. The man fancied himself as something of a hunter, with human lives as his prey. As he stalked through the then-peaceful woods of Ohio, targeting another man for no reason whatsoever, Dillon was unknowingly headed down a path from which he would never return.

Dillon had no reason for targeting his first victim, but it unleashed in him a new type of bloodlust he had never before experienced. As he drove through the back roads of his home state, he began to hear voices nagging at the back of his mind, spurring him into action. One of the voices told him to kill, and he listened with no regrets. When he found Welling jogging along the side of the road, he knew he had found his prey.

He pulled up next to the jogger and leaned out the car window. In his later accounts to the police, Dillon recalled that Welling had casually asked him "what's up?" as if he was attempting to make conversation with the stranger who had been following him down the road. Dillon did not give Welling any sort of reply, but pulled out his sniper rifle and fired. Welling had been merely trying to be friendly just moments before Dillon opened fire on his first of many victims. He shot Welling at point-blank range, from only a few feet away, and remembered it calmly as he related the story to Ohio officials, years later. He stated that it only took ten seconds from the time when the man greeted him until he was dead on the ground, and Dillon never once felt any remorse for taking the life of the unsuspecting jogger. The bullet pierced Welling's heart, and the jogger died almost immediately on a warm Saturday morning in the middle of the Ohio springtime.

After the murder, Dillon simply drove away in his truck, convinced that he had gotten away with a murder that would never be solved. Because he had been lost in his own imagination for so long that day, he managed to drive around a hundred miles away from his home town. He had gunned down a jogger who had no ties to him whatsoever, and disposed of the rifle in an undisclosed location. Although the murder had not been premeditated in the general sense of the word, Dillon was already well on his way to becoming a practiced serial killer. He knew how to behave calmly and surprisingly rationally in the wake of taking another man's life, and as he returned back to his wife and son at home, he barely let the thought of the dead man one hundred miles away cross his mind.

For many years, Dillon got away with Welling's murder as Ohio officials struggled to make a connection between the man's death and any potential suspect. No one had witnessed the murder, and no one had even so much as seen Dillon's truck on the quiet back roads. Since the murder took place on a Saturday morning, the town was still and peaceful, and there had been no one bustling about to catch any sign of what had happened. It would be another several months before Dillon killed again, but as he continued about his ordinary life after gunning down Welling, he would repeatedly find himself drawn to the concept of killing. During this time, Dillon began taking the lives of animals in an attempt to stave off the voices in his head. He found himself lighting fires and shooting pets, and he began to grow more and more violent in his home life. Still, at this point, no one suspected that he could be capable of murder.

Second Murder

The second of Dillon's murders took place in November of 1990, quite a while after Welling's death in April of 1989. Although once again, Dillon had no premeditated reason for going after his second victim, he found himself repeating very similar circumstances that had cropped up during his first murder. The day began much like that fateful day in April had, as Dillon climbed into his truck and stopped for a beer. He then returned to his leisurely Saturday morning drive, getting lost in his thoughts as he so often did, and fantasizing about being someone he was not. Soon, he had gone deeply into his mental world once again, and believed that he had some sort of deed he must carry out. The voices were back, and they were telling him to kill again.

This time, the victim matched almost none of the descriptions of Dillon's previous target. Twenty-one-year-old Jamie Paxton had chosen this particular Saturday morning to get in some hunting in the back woods of Ohio. He headed out without a care in the world, unknowing that he was soon going to become a target himself. In later accounts, Dillon would reiterate time and again that he had never met Jamie Paxton, and that Paxton meant nothing to him as he searched the countryside for someone to gun down. Although the voices were telling him to take another life, Dillon had almost no way of controlling who his victim would be next.

Although there were relatively no connections between Paxton and Dillon's previous victim, Paxton was walking alone just like Welling had been on that similar Saturday morning long before. Had Paxton not chosen to take a walk after his morning hunt, things might have gone differently. Fatefully, he also chose to leave his hunting bow behind in the car, rendering him defenseless to an attack from the now-delusional Dillon. Hoping to enjoy a late morning stroll through the grass near his favorite hunting spot, Paxton left his vehicle on the side of the road and went walking by himself. He would never return. By this time, Dillon had begun to see his victims as prey, and to treat them as though he was hunting for a deer in the woods. He parked some distance down the road from Paxton's vehicle, and stalked Paxton quietly in the tall grasses surrounding the woods. This time, he aimed for the man's head, but ended up firing a total of three shots into his victim before fleeing the scene and once again disposing of the murder weapon. Shooting three times would ultimately lead to the investigation for a serial killer. Had Dillon only shot once, the murder might have been dismissed as an unfortunate hunting accident. Since there were several wounds, however, police realized that this was a murder, and later began connecting the dots to the other, similarly unsolved murder that took place in Ohio some time before.

Nevertheless, at the time of the shooting, there was nothing to connect Dillon to what had just transpired, and he knew it. He was not afraid, and felt no guilt as he packed up following the death of Paxton. After the murder had been carried out, Dillon simply climbed back into his truck and once again drove away, just as he had after gunning down Welling some time before. He drove down the street, picked up a beer, and began making his way back home, with almost no memory of what he had done. Eventually, remorse began to catch up to him in some small way, as he typed a letter recounting the episode and sent it anonymously to the local newspaper, police, and family of the victim. In the letter, he specifically states that he had no guilt over taking the other man's life, but that he did, at that point, see himself as a serial killer. Although the letter repeats that Dillon felt nothing during or after the murder, it is interesting to note that he did at least feel some small obligation to contact the officials about his actions. Although this letter led the police to realize they were dealing with a serial killer, it offered no more clues as to the whereabouts of the man who was taking so many innocent lives on peaceful Saturday mornings in the heart of Southern Ohio.

Third Murder

It would not be much longer before Dillon committed his third murder. In the same month, thirty-year-old Kevin Loring was gunned down in a very similar manner, and Dillon officially entered into the rankings of the textbook serial killer. Technically, to be labeled as a serial killer, a murderer must commit at least three murders, usually with some space in between each. Up until Loring's death, Dillon still had the chance to back out of this lifestyle, but it was far too late for him. He had gotten a taste for blood, and now, there was only one way to satisfy it. Choosing victims so close to one another, however, was a mistake that Dillon would be careful not to make again.

For the third time, Dillon's day began on a warm morning, although it was a Wednesday this time. Unlike all of the other murders Dillon would commit during his stint as a serial killer, this one did not take place on a Saturday, but instead fell during one of Dillon's vacations from work. Just as he had with Paxton, Dillon simply woke up that day and decided that he needed to take another man's life. This was only eighteen days after his previous murder, which would surely leave a more obvious trail between his victims. However, if Dillon realized this, he made no sign of it as he once again got into his red truck and began driving down the road, deeply entranced by his own mental images.

This time, he had awakened with the thought of murder on his mind. He had been unable to shake the voices as they once again directed him to action, and he could do nothing but agree to their demands as he searched for his next victim. By this point, he had gotten quite good at what he did, and he knew what to look for. He knew his victims needed to be people walking alone, in secluded areas without any witnesses nearby to cause problems. He knew that he needed to go far away from his hometown to find them, and that he should also be able to dispose of his murder weapon quickly after fleeing the scene.

Loring's murder was chosen at random just like Dillon's previous two victims had been, but it was a considerably more premeditated event.

Kevin Loring, the unsuspecting third victim, had set out that Saturday morning with some of his friends for a hunting trip. The group had been visiting from Massachusetts, and did not actually call Ohio home. They had come for the excellent hunting in the southern part of the state, but had no idea what fate was about to befall one of their number. After spending the morning hunting together in the woods, the group of friends sat down to enjoy some lunch before heading back home. Loring decided, however, that it was time he got back to his favorite hobby, and began trekking across the open fields of the Ohio countryside on his own. He was working his way back toward some of the better game in the area, but unfortunately, he never arrived at his destination.

As Loring made his way across the fields, his attention was focused almost solely on the task at hand. He was so busy looking for game that he did not begin to realize that he was being stalked himself, by a man in a red truck. Dillon had parked his vehicle some distance away and, much like he had with his previous victim, he began quietly following Loring at a safe shooting distance. By now, Dillon knew much more about making his kills, and he knew what it would take to finish the man off more cleanly than he had the last time. He knew that he needed to pay close attention to where he aimed, much like he would have done if he happened to be hunting deer. He took Loring down with only one shot, straight to his head.

Although Dillon continued to commit his murders in different counties throughout Southern Ohio, they would eventually be connected. At the time of Loring's murder, however, authorities ruled the death as a hunting accident, despite the fact that Loring's companions on the hunting trip had neither seen nor heard anything that would lead them to believe that was what had happened. The answer was not a satisfying one, but it was the best the Ohio authorities had at the time. Dillon once again got away with murder, as he cruised back home in his red truck.

Fourth Murder

It would be another several months before Dillon felt the call to commit murder tug at the back of his mind once again. During his downtime, he returned back to his home and continued about his life as normal, more or less. Looking back on their time with Dillon after his arrest and conviction, his friends and family would start to note subtle changes that were taking place in the man they had once known during the space between his third and fourth murders. However, at the time, nothing seemed terribly out of place, and Dillon continued to fly under the radar of Ohio police, who were still on the lookout for the killer who had taken three lives on three separate occasions across the southern portion of their beloved state.

In March of 1992, Dillon awoke once again with the urge to kill clawing at his mind. This time, as with every other instance before, he wasted no time in getting his gun and heading out to his red truck, intent on finding the perfect victim. He had learned much from his previous experiences. He knew how to choose the right victim, and how to be sure that he shot his target in just the right way so as to take them down in one hit. Although he hoped to cover his tracks by killing his victims with a single bullet, he also may have felt a twinge of remorse or, at the very least, mercy for them. In his letter to the newspaper regarding Jamie Paxton, Dillon had mentioned shooting the young man three times in order to be sure he was completely dead. He even took note of his own nerves as he shot the second time and missed his mark, hitting Paxton in the knee. Killing his victims with one shot likely made it easier for Dillon to process and to black out what he had done, knowing that he had given them, at the least, a swift death. He was prepared to do the same during his fourth murder.

That Saturday morning, Claude Hawkins, a 49-year-old man with a good job, a wife, and four children, clocked out after his long night shift and decided to take in a little fishing before heading home. This was a common practice of his, and his family knew to expect him a little bit later on Saturdays when the urge to go fishing struck. Hawkins thought that the fish were easier to catch in the early mornings, and so rarely missed an opportunity to participate in his favorite pastime after a long week of work. This day was no different, but it soon would take a drastic turn for the worse.

The delusional Dillon drove a long way, as he usually did, and made certain not to enter into any counties that had previously housed his victims. He knew better than to make any connections with his earlier murders as he searched for the perfect fourth target. Keeping his eyes peeled for anyone who might be outdoors in a secluded area far from any witnesses, Dillon soon came across Hawkins' car parked on the side of the road near his favorite fishing spot. Like always, Dillon climbed out of his truck and pursued the man on foot, stalking quietly behind him until he had the perfect shot. He took Hawkins down with one bullet, and fled the scene yet again. He had pulled off his fourth murder without so much as batting an eyelash.

Dillon did not realize, however, that this murder had taken place on government-owned property, which turned the hunt for the killer into a matter of federal importance. With the FBI now involved, authorities from the other three Ohio counties where the previous murders had taken place joined with federal agents to try to work out the mystery of why these lone outdoor adventurers were being gunned down by a mysterious sniper. Unfortunately, not even the FBI had much to go on, as Dillon had covered his tracks well. There were no footprints or fingerprints found at the scene of any of the four crimes, nor were there any shell casings remaining on the ground after the rifles had been fired. It was impossible for agents to so much as track down the murder weapon, much less find any leads as to who was perpetrating these crimes. However, all that was about to change.

Fifth Murder

As the FBI and the Ohio authorities began to study the elements of the four previous murders, Dillon had no idea that they were also starting to form some connections between the events that had transpired over the course of the past four years. The FBI managed to piece together a rudimentary criminal profile that would eventually help lead to the capture of the serial killer the Ohio authorities now realized they were dealing with. At the same time, both teams worked tirelessly to find any shred of evidence that might help them locate the person behind these awful crimes. They begin to provide more information to the public in the hopes that someone might come forward with a lead that could help them solve this deadly mystery.

Meanwhile, Dillon was already feeling the urge to kill rising in the back of his mind once again. By this point, he was well aware that there were voices telling him to do these things, and that he should not be killing other people. However, he still felt little to no remorse for what he did, and his home life began to falter quite a lot more as well. It was around this time that he began to go hunting with a friend of his, who started to take note of Dillon's wild behavior. Dillon began to find more and more reasons to kill animals outside of hunting season, and his friend and hunting companion did not let these warning signs go unheeded. However, he still had no idea that Dillon was planning to commit his fifth murder in April of 1992.

Dillon's final murder took place on a Saturday, as all but one of his previous shootings had as well. Once again, he made his way into a different county, a long way from his home. He drove further than he had before, and felt as though he was covering his tracks perfectly as he yet again scoped out the side of the road for any car that might be parked there alone. He knew exactly what to look for, and wasted no time in finding it as he guzzled one of many of that day's beers from behind the steering wheel of his trusty truck. When he located a vehicle that looked like it fit the bill, he returned to stalking on foot, pretending once more that he was a special operations soldier on the battlefield, looking to take down an enemy for the glory of himself and his country.

That morning, forty-four-year-old West Virginia resident Gary Bradley had decided, perhaps against the wishes of his friends and family who had surely heard about the serial killings taking place in Ohio, to visit his neighboring state and take part in some of the excellent fishing that could be found in one of its many rural counties. He was in the wrong place at the wrong time, fishing from the banks of a large pond, when Dillon came across his vehicle parked a short distance away on the side of the road. Bradley would soon become Dillon's fifth and final victim.

As Dillon trudged through the sparse vegetation, trying not to make a sound while approaching Bradley from the rear, he told himself that he was doing something heroic. He knew he was taking these innocent human lives for a reason, and although the voices might have been unclear on what that reason was, he had to obey them. He lined Bradley up in the sights of his trusty sniper rifle, and knocked him off of his feet with the first blow. Since he could not be sure, from his distance, that he had killed the man, he fired a second shot despite his reluctance to do so. It was better, in Dillon's mind, to leave a longer trail of bullets than it was to leave a victim behind to suffer—and, perhaps, to identify him or his truck in the future. Although there were no witnesses to Bradley's murder, the FBI and Ohio authorities were finally beginning to piece together the puzzle of this bizarre series of outdoor murders. Dillon did not realize it yet, but he had committed his last crime.

Capture

With a fifth murder taking place just a few short days after the fourth, the FBI realized that it was time to make a significant move toward catching the criminal who was running rampant in the woods of Ohio. They began to work much more diligently on their behavioral profile of the serial killer, and to make this information even more available to the public. Although the criminal profile was not spot-on, it would eventually help lead to the capture of Thomas Lee Dillon.

Dillon attempted to commit yet another murder shortly after his fifth, but made the mistake of taking on two men at once. The two men were startled and responded loudly to Dillon's presence in the woods behind them, causing him to flee to his truck. The men did not see him, but did see his vehicle, and reported it to the local authorities immediately. Unfortunately, this was not enough to capture Dillon alone, and the FBI was left with almost no leads once again. However, the tables were about to turn on this deadly situation.

Part of the FBI's profile specified that the serial killer might become violent toward animals or even to his family members. This was one of the first clues that led Richard Fry, one of Dillon's old high school friends, to begin to suspect his friend of something more malicious than simply strange behavior. Fry reported that, even in their much younger days, he had noticed Dillon exhibiting bizarre tendencies. He told the authorities that Dillon had been fond of killing animals, even family pets, and setting fires for no reason when he was younger.

Fry also reported a meeting with Dillon much more recently, which had led to a very uncomfortable exchange between the two men. Just like in their younger days, they had ridden together in Dillon's truck, cruising through Southern Ohio on the lookout for birds and small game to hunt. However, along the way, Dillon had begun asking Fry some very peculiar questions. He asked his old friend if he ever thought about killing other people, and even went so far as to question Fry on whether or not he himself came across as a serial killer. He discussed at length how easy it would be to cover his tracks simply by killing victims in different counties, and how such a tactic would surely slow down any investigations. By the time Fry parted ways with his strange old high school buddy, he knew there was something seriously wrong going on. When he heard the police report and the detailed behavioral profile of the serial killer they were hunting, he was certain that he had found their man.

Soon after, the FBI began to investigate their only significant suspect, Thomas Lee Dillon. Investigators noted that Dillon had been available and free from work on every date on which a murder had taken place, and this was enough to lead the FBI to trail Dillon every day, just out of his sight. They followed along behind him through the back roads as he made his frequent trips throughout the surrounding Ohio counties. Dillon was eventually caught on tape visiting the gravesite of Jamie Paxton, but even still, this was not enough to prove his ultimate guilt. Finally, the FBI managed to convince Dillon that he had been captured on all counts of murder, in the hopes of making him confess of his own free will. The police had no way to know for sure that their plan would work, and unfortunately, it initially failed. In the end, however, investigators were able to find ballistic evidence that linked Dillon to his most recent murder, and the pieces of the puzzle started to fall into place. With a link to Dillon's rifle, there was now irrefutable proof of his guilt in the murders. With so much evidence being shoved in his face, Dillon eventually took a negotiation that kept him from receiving the death penalty provided he confessed to all five murders. Finally, Thomas Lee Dillon was sentenced to life in prison on five counts of murder, and this horrifying chapter in Ohio's history was able to come to a close.

TERMINATOR : THE TRUE STORY OF ANATOLY ONOPRIENKO

"I'm an angel who was attending a school of Satan. Some will call me schizophrenic or even Hitler or other terrible things. That's okay with me."
- Anatoly Onoprienko

CHAPTER ONE

Anatoly Onoprienko was born in the village of Lasky in Zhtomyr Oblast in the Ukraine on July 25th, 1959. His father, Yuri Onoprienko, was a World War II hero for the Soviet Union but according to Anatoly he was abusive and an alcoholic. He also had a younger brother who was thirteen years older than him.

His mother died when he was four years old and his father sent him to live with his grandparents and aunt. The grandparents subsequently sent him to an orphanage.

Onoprienko became bitter at his family and father for sending him to the orphanage. His older brother was allowed to stay in the family home while he was sent away.

"I remember my father and brother staring at me," Onoprienko said recalling his youth. "Staring at me saying, 'let's send him to an orphanage.' I don't blame them but I'm horrified by their memory. I remember their voices."

It is unknown why Anatoly was sent to the orphanage alone while his brother remained in the care of his father. His grandmother stayed with him for the first few days there, helping him to adjust. She would eventually leave but would visit often and bring care packages of food.

A shy and quiet young boy, he did manage to make friends inside the orphanage. He would play soccer and other sports. His grades began to decline, however, as he entered the college of forestry at age fourteen.

Teachers noted a shift in his personality and became concerned. He began drinking Vodka like his father and became involved in petty thefts.

Onoprienko left the college of forestry at the age of seventeen, still unsure of what to do with his life. He joined the army in 1976 and it is here where he mastered the use of firearms. Instead of becoming a good soldier, however, he became even more alienated.

"When I was twenty years old I called myself stupid because I couldn't understand people," Onoprienko recalled. "If they were smart then I must be stupid."

Onoprienko was discharged from the army then became a sailor. He gained employment on a cruise ship in Odessa and where he would often steal money from cabins. Despite his anti-social temperament, Onoprienko had a handful of girlfriends that he would try to impress with gifts purchased with money he had stolen.

One waitress on the cruise ship caught his eye and the two began dating. She would remain his girlfriend for three years and she would give birth to his first child. Onoprienko would take a stab at being a father for awhile but discovered that it wasn't for him.

Without a word, he left his girlfriend and his baby. Onoprienko would never see them again.

"I had a unique destiny," Onoprienko said. "I had to go out and find it. I felt restless at home. Stifled. Married life wasn't for me. I needed something more."

That "something more" would be crime and murder.

CHAPTER TWO

"Onoprienko's criminal activity would increase in 1989," Ruslan Moshkovsky (Onoprienko's attorney) said. "The USSR was collapsing and no one was responsible for anything."

Onoprienko's first murder would start with his landlady.

He broke into her apartment with the goal of stealing a few pieces of jewelry. The landlady, however, came home and demanded to know what he was doing in her house.

Onoprienko panicked and shot the woman dead.

He ran out of the apartment and continued on with his life as usual. Because the police resources were so stretched out, Onoprienko was never even questioned in the murder and the crime would remain unsolved.

Onoprienko would team up with a fellow petty thief, Sergei Rogozin, and the duo would break into various residences around Kiev.

Returning home from a night of thievery, the two spotted a car pulling a trailer late one night. Onoprienko sped in front of the vehicle, blocking its route then jumped out of his car with a sawed-off shotgun in hand.

A young couple was inside and Onoprienko fired upon them without warning.

"What are you doing?" Rogozin screamed.

"Shut up!"

"I thought we were just going to rob them."

Onoprienko sprang up in Rogozin's face, caressing his cheek with the barrel of his shotgun. "If you don't shut up...If you say anything, I will kill your entire family and make you watch. Do you understand?"

Rogozin could only nod his head in agreement.

Onoprienko then buried the bodies of the couple and set fire to their car.

A month later, the two thieves gunned down another couple using the same method. Onoprienko would speed in front of the car and stop. His victims caught unaware and defenseless, Onoprienko would spring out of his car and blast away.

Rogozin would say nothing and just take whatever valuables he could find off the victims.

Onoprienko would continue accumulating his victims in this manner. He would stop families on abandoned roads and kill everyone inside. Even children.

The home burglaries continued as well with Rogozin. Onoprienko killed a family of ten people when he and Rogozin were caught in the midst of robbing their house. Two adults and eight children were killed by the duo. Onoprienko then ceased all ties with Rogozin.

"He was a kind, intelligent man," Rogozin would say later of Onoprienko. "He wasn't greedy. He seemed good-natured. I cannot say anything bad about him."

CHAPTER THREE

Onoprienko kept a low profile for a few years, moving in with a distant cousin. There are six years in his life that are unaccounted for. Some say he spent some time in a mental institution while others insist that he may be responsible for more crimes in and around the former Soviet Union. He tried to get asylum in Western Europe but failed, returning to his native Ukraine.

"He worked in Germany and Austria," Dmitry Lipsky, the trial judge said. "During our interrogation we asked if he had killed anyone there. He denied it. He said he had only committed a robbery."

"At the very beginning, I had an option to commit suicide," Onoprienko said. "And to stop this mission to kill. But then with the passage of time there was an order from above that I cannot kill myself. I'm supposed to live and keep doing what I'm doing and finish this game."

Onoprienko would return to the Ukraine in 1985 and begin a killing rampage the likes of which his country had never seen. He had anticipated that his crimes on the highway would become the stuff of legend. Instead, they were forgotten in a bureaucratic quagmire.

Not only were his crimes unknown to the general public, no one was even investigating them.

The Soviet Union had collapsed and his native state, the Ukraine, was now an independent country.

"When he came back," Moshkovsky said. "And realized that everything had been forgotten and no one was looking for him, he embarked on his second killing spree."

Like a shark circling around a minnow of fish, Onoprienko moved from town to town surveying the lay of the land. He visited some relatives who were hunters and stole a shotgun from them.

Onoprienko would saw off the barrel of the gun in order to cause maximum damage. He wanted not only to kill again but to gain notoriety for the murders.

His new crime wave started with a seventy year old woman in Odessa. He broke into her home, shot her dead then set the home on fire.

"My main purpose wasn't to rob," Onoprienko said. "My purpose was cruel. I can't explain it. My purpose was to threaten people and threaten the police. And lead them in the wrong direction."

Days later, he would travel to a town called Malyn. He skulked around the town at night and come upon a young couple having sex in their car.

"I shot at them from the driver side," Onoprienko said. "I wounded the man then the woman jumped out of the car. I waited until she put her clothes on. Then she ran off. Probably to get some help."

The woman returned shortly thereafter to check on her lover. With Onoprienko hiding near the car, he stabbed her to death. He put the woman in the car, shot the man again then drove to a secluded area where he set the car on fire.

"I started realizing that there was a plan for me," Onoprienko said. "Something was giving me direction."

CHAPTER FOUR

Onoprienko began targeting families that lived in isolated areas around Kiev. He would follow the same modus operandi in each killing. He would create a distraction, usually throwing a brick through the front window to lure the adult male(s) out of the home. Then he would kill the man of the house before entering the home and killing the wife, saving the children for last. He would then set the house on fire in order to remove all evidence. There were instances wherein witnesses would cross his path and he would kill them as well.

Onoprienko was a nocturnal killer. During the day, he played the role of the down on his luck blue collar worker but at night he would seek out fame by being a serial killer.

He would move to a town called Yavoriv, moving in with a cousin named Pyotr and his wife Yelena. Ukrainian families were communal in nature and Pyotr saw it as his duty to take care of his struggling cousin.

Pyotr's wife Yelena, however, didn't like Onoprienko. She knew that there was something 'off' about the man and felt uneasy when she discovered the rifle under his bed.

Yelena pressured her husband into kicking Onoprienko out of the house. Pyotr could not throw his cousin out on the streets but he decided instead to play matchmaker. He knew a hair dresser that was recently divorced and looking for a decent man to be her meal ticket. Pyotor threw a family party, invite the woman over and she immediately hit it off with Onoprienko.

The woman was named Ana Kazak. She had two children of her own but her ex-husband was an alcoholic. She an attraction to the soft-spoken Onoprienko and the two began living together.

Onoprienko told his new live-in girlfriend that he was a "traveling businessman" and she never questioned his long absences from home.

Onoprienko would travel all the way to Malyn which was a town that was often hit by blackouts. He would be able to get in and out, do his killings under the cloak of night when no one had electricity nor did they have the capability to call for help. It was the perfect scenario for the serial killer.

CHAPTER FIVE

It was Christmas Eve when Onoprienko came upon the secluded home of the Zaichenko family which was located in the small village of Garmarnia. Inside, a forestry teacher lived along with his wife and two sons.

Onoprienko crept around the exterior of the home, found a ladder and propped it against the wall. He climbed up to the bedroom window and fired through the glass, killing the father and three year old son who was sleeping with him.

"I just shot them," Onoprienko said. "It's not that it gave me pleasure, but I felt this urge. From then on, it was almost like some game from outer space."

Onoprienko then jumped through the window and went from room to room.

"Don't kill us!" the wife pleaded as Onoprienko came through her door. He stabbed the woman and then strangled their three-month old baby.

"I didn't want to waste bullets on the weak," Onoprienko said.

He then ripped the wedding rings off the couple's hands as well as taking a small golden cross on a chain, earrings and clothes before torching the home.

Onoprienko would later say that he had "a vision from God" and was ordered to murder.

"When we arrived at the site, we were in shock," Leonid Martynenko, lead investigator of the Zaichenko murder said. "We discovered that the whole family had died violently. At the time, we didn't know the reason for the crime. We developed leads, examined a number of options. We considered burglary the main motive then. We thought it was homicide for purpose of robbery."

Onoprienko returned home and spent Christmas with Ana and her two sons. On New Year's Eve, however, the told her that he had to "go away on business."

Onoprienko would then travel to the town of Bratkovichi where he would indulge in his killing fantasies once again.

The streets of the town were deserted at night and Onoprienko was getting antsy. Then in the distance, he saw a man walking down the street.

"How you doing?" Onoprienko asked the man. "Was wondering if you could spare me a dollar or two so I can get something to eat?"

"Get the fuck away from me, you bum!" the man said. He was dressed in a forestry uniform and looked to be going home from work.

"Just a dollar."

"Fuck you!"

The man turned around and Onoprienko shot him in the back. The forester fell face first to the ground. Onoprienko quickly dragged the man to the side of the road. He rifled through his pockets, taking his money and keys. Then he stripped the man naked.

The night was just getting started for Onoprienko as he continued his rampage throughout the town. He noticed a man hanging curtains in his window and Onoprienko fired away, killing the man. Breaking into the home, he killed the man's wife and her twin sisters that were also living there. He then cut off the wife's finger and stole her wedding ring.

"It was like cutting through a tree branch," Onoprienko said. "It was very easy. Cutting through flesh was like cutting through butter."

He could not help but stop to admire his handiwork before he set the house ablaze.

"I was observing the victims," Onoprienko said. "Those who were already killed. How they were killed or were dying. Or how they were living the last minutes of their lives."

Onoprienko hopped on the train and returned home. When he got home, he took the wedding ring off the dead woman's finger and proposed to Ana.

"After the second murder we knew we had a maniac on our hands," Martynenko said. "We came to the location and viewed the scene. We saw the brutality of the crime and it had become absolutely clear to us that it was the same man that committed all the killings."

Gathering and sharing information still proved to be a problem in the Ukraine. Old Soviet style narratives were still being adhered to, like that of the government never admitting that serial killers existed in their country. It was part of the old Soviet style propaganda, wanting to prove to the world that killings didn't take place in their Communist territory. Even though the Ukraine was now free from such commandments, the leadership still adhered to keeping information away from the public and not admitting that they had a problem.

"It was striking how systematic the murders were," Romanyuk said. "There were group murders. Whole families were wiped out for no visible reason. That was really astounding."

Four days later after his marriage proposal, Onoprienko began gunning people down on the Berdyansk, Dnieprovskaya highway. He stopped cars, feigning as if he needed assistance then he would shoot the drivers. The victims were Kasai, a Navy ensign, a taxi driver named Savitsky, a kolkhoz cook named Kochergina and another unidentified victim.

"To me it was like hunting," Onoprienko said. "Hunting people down. I would be sitting, bored, with nothing to do. And then suddenly this idea would get into my head. I would do everything to get it out of my mind, but I couldn't. It was stronger than me. So I would get in the car or catch a train and go out to kill."

Onoprienko waited another eleven days, take a train to the village of Bratkovichi and invading the home of the Pilat family. He would shoot all five family members in the home and once again set fire to the place. He would be seen by two witnesses and he promptly killed them both.

"I look at it very simply," Onoprienko said. ""As an animal, I watched all this as an animal would stare at sheep."

The blood lust now running freely, Onoprienko could not refrain himself from killing.

On January 30th, 1996, Onoprienko killed a nurse named Marusina, her two sons and a family friend in Fastova, Kieskaya Oblast region of the Ukraine.

"I could not stop myself," he would say later to investigators. "I became obsessed with killing. To me killing people is like ripping up a duvet. Men, women, old people, children, they are all the same. I have never felt sorry for those I killed. No love, no hatred, just blind indifference. I don't see them as individuals, but just as masses."

Onoprienko would continue to take small items from the homes as souvenirs before going back home. He would bring his fiancee clothes, jewelry and a tape deck which he presented as gifts.

On February 19th , 1996, Onoprienko invaded the home of the Dubchak family. He shot and killed the father and son then bludgeoned the mother to death with a hammer. The family had a daughter, and he walked into her room to find her praying.

"Where do your parents keep the money!" he demanded.

The girl looked at her killer straight in the eye, defiant.

"Show me where the money is!"

"No, I won't," the girl said.

Onoprienko then killed the girl.

'That strength (the girl's) was incredible," Onoprieko said. "But I felt nothing."

Onoprienko then broke into the home of the Bodnarchuck family in Malina, Lvivskaya Oblast. He started with his usual tactic of throwing a rock at the door. The father, however, came out of the home with an ax. Onoprienko promptly shot the man and then the wife who came to the door to investigate the noise. Onoprienko then went inside and chopped up the daughters with the ax. A neighbor named Tsalk wandered onto the property and Onoprienko shot him to death before chopping up his body as well.

"Oh, you know, I killed them because I loved them so much," Onoprienko said. "Those children, those men and women, I had to kill them, the inner voice spoke inside my mind and heart and pushed me so hard!"

On March 22nd, 1996, Onoprienko shot and killed members of the Novosad family. He then set the house on fire to remove all traces of evidence.

"He would always set the places on fire," Romanyuk said. "People saw the fire and came to fight it. There was no evidence left only holes in the walls and cartridges."

Police would use forensic science to discover that the holes in the walls were left by a hunting weapon, specifically a gun that had the barrel sawed off.

"I'm not a maniac," Onoprienko said. "If I were, I would have thrown myself onto you and killed you right here. No, it's not that simple. I have been taken over by a higher force, something telepathic or cosmic, which drove me. I am like a rabbit in a laboratory. A part of an experiment to prove that man is capable of murdering and learning to live with his crimes. To show that I can cope, that I can stand anything, forget everything."

The Ukrainian government could no longer keep a lid on the killings. Rumors had spread of a man who was on a rampage throughout the entire country, murdering families at random.

The people of the region all lived in fear. Some families would stay together at night and press their furniture up against the door at night.

"People would come home from work early," said one Ukrainian resident. "People were scared to death. Students who were away at college quickly came home to be with their parents. I had one neighbor that put bars on their windows. Everyone was scared."

The press had given him the nickname of "The Terminator."

Onoprienko had achieved his goal. He had become the most feared man in his country.

CHAPTER SIX

The Ukrainian military patrolled certain villages to keep the people safe. Schools near the murders were shut down as a precaution. There was daily radio updates and a lot of the citizens likened the experience to being in a war.

"All the police departments were given specific instructions as to what to look for," Romanyuk said. "They knew how the killer behaved, that he acted at night. They investigated any sound. Even when a dog barked at night. The orders were strict."

The Ukraine launched a sweeping manhunt, determined to find the killer. They were convinced that this was the work of one man and dispensed their National Guard plus over 2,000 police investigators on the case.

"We had special teams of different officers working in different capacities," Bodgan Romanyuk, the chief of police said. "We had officers in the field, around-the-clock gathering information and working with operatives. Then there were others who in charge of strategy, who conducted the ground operations."

Later that month, the Security Service of Ukraine (SBU) and the Public Prosecutor's Office specialists arrested a 26-year old man named Yury Mozola, thinking he was responsible for the family murders. Over the course of three days, seven Ukrainian law enforcement officials tortured the young man, employing burning, electrocution and beatings.

Mozola, however, refused to confess and would later die during the torture.

The seven men were then prosecuted for the murder and sentenced to jail.

Days later after Mozola's death, Onoprienko was finally captured after a massive manhunt.

An anonymous caller gave police a tip on Onoprienko. He said that he witnessed him trying to conceal a shotgun as he left his apartment building.

Police then surrounded Onoprienko's building, staking out every possible exit until storming the apartment.

"It was quite risky," Romanyuk said. "Because on the one hand there was no evidence. But, on the other hand, what if it's him? What if it is this trained killer who shoots people dead on the spot and our officers are only human."

"We had learned that our suspect was anti-social. He wouldn't open the door to anyone. It was Easter and his fiance went to visit her mother, out of town. She would return in the evening and when we rang we'd hope that he'd think that it was her coming home."

The police came to the door and knocked.

Opening the door was a small man with red hair.

He opened the door calmly, expecting his girlfriend.

The police forced their way in and demanded his identification.

Onoprienko then reached for his gun but the police overpowered him, grabbing his wrists. Wresting the pistol away, they identified it as one that had been stolen from a crime scene.

Searching the man for his identification, they recognized him as Anatoly Onoprienko.

"In the apartment is everything," Romanyuk said. "All the evidence is there. Things from the crime scenes where he murdered people in different regions."

The police officers held up the numerous guns and knives to his face.

"It isn't mine!" the killer protested. "All that stuff doesn't belong to me."

His fiancee Ana, return home. She was shocked to see Onoprienko being arrested as she maintained that he had been the sweetest man she had ever met and had been nothing but nice to her and her two children.

The police, however, disputed her notions by showing her the weapons that he had stashed in her apartment.

"I started talking with his fiancee," Romanyuk recalled. "And I tried to find ways of connecting him with these murders. We were able to match dates. She would give us a date when he wasn't home for a day or two and that date would correspond with the murders."

The police searched through the apartment and found over one-hundred twenty-two items that were taken from the crime scenes. Guns and knives all matched what they were looking for in terms of murder weapons.

After the debacle with the previous suspect, the police authorities wanted proof beyond a shadow of a doubt.

"For me," Romanyuk said. "It was crucial that it we were sure that it was him. To make sure that he could be tied to these killings."

The police brought the killer into the station and interrogated him until six o'clock in the morning. Onoprienko denied all involvement until he finally cracked early in the morning.

"I was commanded by God to kill," Onoprienko told his interrogators. "I was chosen because I'm a superior specimen. I have the power of hypnosis and can call animals through telepathy. I can stop and start my heart with my mind."

He told of being diagnosed with schizophrenia and being admitted to a hospital in Kiev.

"He told us about all fifty-two murders he committed," Romanyuk said. "Not only the ones he performed in 1995 but also about the murders he committed in the past a long time ago."

Onoprienko expressed relief at being caught. He had grew tired of killing and being covered in blood all the time.

The police then turned Onoprienko over to the Ukrainian interior ministry.

Upon his transference to this higher authority, Onoprienko immediately began making demands.

"Give me a box of candy," Onoprienko said. "Sausages and some crackers. Otherwise I won't talk to you."

Onoprienko was then allowed to take advantage of a strange quirk in Ukrainian law. In the Ukraine, a trial cannot commence until the defendant has read all of the evidence against him.

At his leisure.

Onoprienko was obligated to read over volumes of police reports and crime scene photos. There were over fifty-two dead bodies, some dismembered and burned. Finally, he relented and after seven months he led the police to the areas where he had killed his victims. Onoprienko would detail each murder with an eery calmness, remarking at how easy it was for him to kill his victims.

There was another delay in that the Ukraine would have to transport, feed and house all of the witnesses who came from different parts of the country. Ultimately, there would be no witnesses testifying at his trial as some of the family members did not want to come forth.

A full three years after his apprehension, Onoprienko was finally brought to trial. Onoprienko was forced to sit in court in an iron cage. People spat upon him and threatened to tear him apart.

"I'm a person, a regular person," Onoprienko said. "Anybody can become a murderer. I was helped. It either it a God or the devil. Whatever he calls himself."

"He needs to be shot!" screamed a woman in the court room.

"He does not deserve to be shot!" screamed another. "He needs to die a slow and agonizing death."

The trial drew national publicity and the security around the courtroom was tight.

Judge Dmytro Lypsky asked Onoprienko if he had anything to say.

"No, nothing," the killer said shrugging his shoulders.

"You have been informed of our legal rights-"

"It's your law," he growled.

"State your nationality," the judge said.

"None."

"That's impossible."

"According to the police," Onoprienko said. "I'm Ukrainian."

"Do you have anything else to say in your defense?"

"I've been a robot for years," the killer said. "Driven by dark forces. I should not be put on trial until authorities can determine the force. You are not able to take me as I am. You do not see all the good I'm going to do! And you will never understand me. This is a great force that controls this hall as well. You will never understand this. Maybe only your grandchildren will understand.

Onoprienko was cooperative throughout the trial until the end. He requested that his state-appointed lawyer, Ruslan Mashkovsky, be replaced by someone who was "at least 50 years old, Jewish or half-Jewish, economically independent and has international experience."

The court refused his request. He was confined to a metal cage inside the courtroom as the rest of the proceedings took place.

"I started preparing for prison life a long time ago," Onoprienko recalled. "I fasted, did yoga, I am not afraid of death," Onoprienko said. "Death for me is nothing. Naturally, I would prefer the death penalty. I have absolutely no interest in relations with people. I have betrayed them. The first time I killed, I shot down a deer in the woods. I was in my early twenties and I recall feeling very upset when I saw it dead. I couldn't explain why I had done it and I felt sorry for it. I never had that feeling again."

The closing arguments began in April of 1999. Prosecutor Yury Ignatenko pressed for the death sentence while Moshkovsky would try to bring up Onoprienko's childhood to generate his sympathy.

"My defendant was deprived of motherly love since the age of four," Moshkovsky argued. "And the absence of care which is necessary for the formation of a real man. I appeal to the court to soften the punishment."

Moshkovsky himself, however, knew that Onoprienko was the epitome of evil, saying and doing things for dramatic effect.

"He was a cunning, shrewd and a great psychologist," Moshkovsky said later. "He was hard to catch because he acted alone and without accomplices. He was a butcher, killing defenseless and poor people. He specifically chose villages on the outskirts where there was no telephone, where even cars pass with difficulty. Even if someone heard a shot, there would be no one to call."

After only three hours of deliberation, the judge sentenced Onoprienko to death by shooting.

"I've robbed and killed," Onoprienko said in his final statement. "But I'm a robot, I don't feel anything. I've been close to death so many times that it's even interesting for me now to venture into the after world, to see what is there, after this death."

The Ukraine, however, had just joined the Council of Europe and had committed to abolishing capital punishment.

Onoprienko was then spared the death penalty even though he gave the President of the Ukraine a personalized letter that he would kill again.

"If I am ever let out, I will start killing again," Onoprienko wrote. "But this time it will be worse, ten times worse. The urge is there. Seize this chance because I am being groomed to serve Satan. After what I have learnt out there, I have no competitors in my field. And if I am not killed I will escape from this jail and the first thing I'll do is find Kuchma (the Ukrainian president) and hang him from a tree by his testicles."

The Terminator would die of heart failure in the prison of Zhytomyr on August 27th, 2013 at the age of 54.

TOY BOX KILLER

NATALIE MARSHALL

David Parker Ray was a suspected American serial killer and known torturer and serial rapist of women; suspected because no bodies were ever found. However, he was accused by his accomplices of murdering a number of women and law enforcement officials estimate that he is responsible for as many as 60 deaths in and near Truth or Consequences, New Mexico. Ray purchased and refitted a trailer into what he called his "toy box" which was replete with a number of sex toys and torture items for his victims. He also played a very disturbing audiotape for all of his victims explaining what they will be enduring at his hand. Ray was finally arrested after one of his victims managed to escape after three days of torture. Ray stood trial for kidnapping and sexual torture and was sentenced to 224 years in prison; however, he suffered a fatal heart attack while incarcerated at Lea County Correctional Facility in Hobbs, New Mexico, on 28 May 2002.

Early Life

David Parker Ray was born on 6 November 1939, in Belen, New Mexico. He was named David after his uncle David who was accidentally shot in the heart at the age of 13 by his 15-year-old brother Alden just one year earlier. Ray's grandmother believed him to be a reincarnation of her dead son.

Ray's father, Cecil, was an alcoholic and was very abusive to both Ray and his sister Peggy—who was one year his junior—as well as their mother, Nettie. When Ray was ten years old his father left his mother and moved to Albuquerque. They were divorced soon thereafter. When Nettie decided to stay with her own parents, Ray and Peggy were shipped off to their paternal grandparents, Ethan and Dolly Ray. In the six years Ray and Peggy lived with their grandparents they saw their father twice and their mother only a handful of times. Consequently, there were no maternal bonds between Nettie and her children. In fact, Ray said that he didn't get much affection or attention at all during his childhood.

Ethan was a strict disciplinarian who insisted on the utmost standards of dress and behavior and, as such, the children were required to do ranch chores both before and after school and even though the Rays were not very well off, Ethan made sure his grandchildren were clean and presentable. He was also a devout fundamentalist Christian and made sure to instill within his grandchildren his religious beliefs. Any nonadherence to his rules resulted in physical punishment.

Ray attended Mountainair High School in Mountainair, New Mexico, where he was often bullied for his awkwardness and shyness, especially around girls. Ray commented that he didn't have his first date until he was 18 years old. He was also tormented for being soft-spoken and for having to keep his shirt buttoned all the way to the top—per his grandfather's instructions—when all of the other boys had a few top buttons undone. Ray was also a poor student.

Neighbor Audie Miranda always tried to look out for Ray. He would tell the bullies to leave him alone and stated that even though Ray could defend himself, he remained docile, not liking or believing in violence which was ironic considering what Ray would become. The two became close friends and spent a lot of time together on the Ray ranch riding horses, playing cowboys and Indians, and playing desert hide-and-seek.

Ray always had a love of the outdoors.

Miranda would later say that he believed that Ray's ultra-strict upbringing took a toll on his friend. Miranda even commented that he, himself, was scared of Ethan.

Dolly was not much better. Ray said that he hated her and that she "didn't have a clue."

At the age of 12, Ray began building and setting off bombs and other explosives he fashioned in the woods behind his grandparents' house. He said he blew up a lot of tree stumps as a child.

When Ray was 13 his grandparents gave him a Cushman Pacemaker motor scooter. He discovered within himself a natural aptitude for mechanics and delighted in taking it apart and then reassembling it. The once shy and timid Ray became more confident, especially when his classmates who used to torment him needed his services to fix their scooters.

Some accounts state that Ray began to use and abuse alcohol and drugs while in high school. It was also around this time he began to fantasize about raping, torturing, and murdering women. He said that the few times his father would come visit them, he would bring true detective magazines which Ray enjoyed reading. He began having his fantasies which always involved broken bottles. His sister stumbled upon Ray's sadomasochistic drawings as well as erotic photographs of acts of bondage.

At the age of 15 Ray fashioned his own little dungeon under a large piñon pine tree with a hangman's noose and a collection of broken beer bottles he "planned to use on girls someday." He also admitted to digging a hole and engaging in intercourse with the ground when he was lonesome.

After high school, Ray worked as an auto mechanic.

He married in 1959, joking that he was practically a virgin at that time, and joined the United States Army a year later where he was sent to Korea. The Rays had a son in 1960 and Ray had to return home on emergency leave because his wife was leaving the baby alone when she went out to party. He filed for divorce and sought sole custody. His mother, Opel, and stepfather, Cecil, raised Ray's son until Ray was honorably discharged from the military.

Ray married a second time in 1962 when he was 22 years old and a mere 90 days later he went back to court and filed for divorce again because they just didn't "click".

In 1966, Ray married a third time; to a woman named Glenda Burdine. They were married 15 years and had a daughter named Glenda Jean—who would go by "Jesse"—in 1969. Jesse remembered her father as being gone quite a bit, having worked for the railroad, and of having an unusual fetish for padded leather straps and other bondage fare. She said that kids were naturally curious and while they knew about it, it was not a topic to be discussed.

In sum, Ray married four times, was divorced four times, and had two children.

Ray met Cindy Lea Hendy in 1997 when he was 57; she was 20 years his junior. Originally from Washington, Hendy and her boyfriend John Youngblood moved to Truth or Consequences, New Mexico, on the run from the law for grand theft, forgery, and drug offenses, leaving her three children behind. As she had already served time in jail, she was not keen on returning.

The Crimes

The "Toy Box"

Ray spent over $100,000 on his homemade torture chamber he called his "toy box" that he constructed inside of an old white 15-feet-by-25-feet cargo trailer on his Elephant Butte, New Mexico, property. Elephant Butte is a resort town of approximately 2,000 residents, located along an 18-mile-long, 36,000-acre reservoir.

The trailer was stocked with what he referred to as his "friends": bully whips, pulleys, leather straps, metal clamps, bars which spread the victim's legs, surgical knifes and saws which he used to torture women. Inside this trailer were also numerous sex toys, syringes, detailed diagrams that showed different methods for inflicting pain and torture, and a homemade electrical generator. Ray also mounted a mirror on the ceiling above the gynecologist table upon which he strapped his victims because he wanted them to see everything that was done to them.

He also played a recorded audiotape of himself for his victims whenever they regained consciousness. It began with:

*"Hello there, b*tch. Are you comfortable right now? I doubt it. Wrists and ankles chained. Gagged. Probably blind folded. You are disoriented*

*and scared, too, I would imagine. Perfectly normal, under the circumstances. For a little while, at least, you need to get your sh*t together and listen to this tape. It is very relevant to your situation. I'm going to tell you, in detail, why you have been kidnapped, what's going to happen to you and how long you'll be here. I don't know the details of your capture, because this tape is being created July 23rd, 1993, as a general advisory tape for future female captives. The information I'm going to give you is based on my experience dealing with captives over a period of several years. If, at a future date, there are any major changes in our procedures, the tape will be upgraded. Now, you are obviously here against your will, totally helpless, don't know where you're at, don't know what's gonna happen to you. You're very scared or very pissed off. I'm sure that you've already tried to get your wrists and ankles loose, and know you can't. Now you're just waiting to see what's gonna happen next."*

The rest of the tape involves Ray setting forth his "rules" and "procedures" by telling his victims everything—in graphic detail—that would be done to them to include being raped and sodomized by Ray and his friends, engaging in bestiality, being shocked with electricity, and being poked and prodded with a multitude of surgical instruments and sex toys; essentially, being their sex slave to do with whatever they want. The actual recording is widely available online, quite long, and not for the faint of heart as it is extremely explicit.

In the audiotape Ray describes himself as a "dungeon master" who was affiliated with the Church of Satan and that his slaves were for members of his "congregation."

There was also a videotape showing Ray and his girlfriend Cindy Lea Hendy performing such acts of torture upon a female victim who screamed the entire time.

Psychological torture was also important to Ray. He would blindfold his victims, subject them to brainwashing, use fear tactics, and occasional small favors to keep them "off balance".

Many experts classify Ray as a sexual sadist who finds excitement and pleasure from inflicting pain upon a nonconsensual, submissive and inducing them into altered states of consciousness such as when they pass out from the pain. Such a predilection often forms during adolescence; however, experts do not know exactly what causes one to become a sexual sadist.

Ray had multiple accomplices during this time; including, allegedly, several of his girlfriends, particularly his latest girlfriend, Hendy.

During the investigation Hendy allegedly had told a friend—while she was under the influence of alcohol—that she had willingly participated in Ray's attacks because of the adrenaline rush she got from them. She allegedly confided to this person that "there were four to six people who had been killed, dismembered, and tossed into Elephant Butte Lake." While the friend did not initially believe her, after Ray and Hendy were arrested and the details of the crimes were released, he gave statements to police and the media.

Marie Parker

On 5 July 1997, 22-year-old Marie Parker and her two daughters—ages four and five—were evicted from their apartment for non-payment of rent. They were living in a pup tent on the western shore of Elephant Butte Lake at a campsite called Hot Springs Cove; just north of Ray's trailer. In fact, she had borrowed the tent from him and when her campsite became too messy for the fastidious Ray, he had something to say about it.

Parker was a methamphetamine and cocaine junkie and her main supplier was Ray's daughter Jesse. Ray abducted Parker and took her to his toy box where he raped and tortured her for three days after which he gave Yancy a rope and told him that they "were finished" with her. He then told Yancy to kill her which Yancy admitted to doing. They buried the body in a remote area and Ray threatened Yancy's life if he ever told anyone.

Later, when police took Yancy to the area where Parker's body was allegedly dumped, they could not find any evidence. Yancy stated that Ray probably moved the body.

Police found Parker's abandoned car in the parking lot of the Blue Waters Saloon.

Cynthia Vigil

Cynthia Vigil had been working as a prostitute along Central Avenue (Highway 66) at around 10:00 a.m. when her pimp introduced her to Ray and Hendy in a red recreational vehicle. Ray offered Vigil $20 for oral sex and when she entered the vehicle, Ray produced a police badge and told Vigil that she was under arrest for solicitation. Ray and Hendy handcuffed, gagged, and chained Vigil to a fixture inside of the camper. After a few minutes he pulled the vehicle over and then proceeded to cut off all of her clothing, put a metal dog collar around her neck, place her in shackles, and then slipped a leather mask over her head with no eye openings and a zipper for the mouth. She was also told if she resisted she would be shocked.

When they reached Ray's house, after driving for an hour, Vigil said that she was chained to a bed and was made to listen to Ray's infamous five-minute audiotape before being forced to have sex with both Ray and Hendy. Next, Vigil said that Ray put gravy "up" her and had his German shepherd lick it off. Vigil then had her knees attached to a bar, forcing her legs open and was then "measured" with dildoes that had markings on them before having her breasts and genitals shocked with a portable generator. The entire time Hendy had a gun pointed at her.

The next morning, Vigil was taken at gunpoint to the bathroom to relieve herself and then taken back to the bed, fresh and clean white sheets atop it, where her mouth and eyes were duct taped and she was hog-tied with an elaborate collection of interconnected leather straps. A rope was then attached to a pulley from the ceiling and Vigil's entire body was lifted three feet into the air.

The duct tape was ripped from her eyes and she saw her horrified face staring back at her from a video monitor. She said that Ray tied her legs open and proceeded to whip her with a leather belt, whips, and a cat-o' nine tails. Vigil said that the beating excited Ray who then violated her with a "horrendous looking dildo" and took pictures of her suspended body with the toys inside of her.

Later that day he attached an elaborate system of clamps and pulleys to her breasts and genitalia and proceeded to shock her. Her convulsions caused the pulleys to exert force on the clamps. After taking the excruciating pain for as long as she could, she lost consciousness.

For the next two days Vigil was subjected to sexual torture until she was able to escape.

On 22 March 1999, Cynthia Vigil escaped after being abducted by Ray and enduring a three-day torture ordeal. She was able to escape one morning after Ray had left for work and Hendy had left the keys on a nearby table when the latter went into another room to talk on the phone. Vigil—chained to the wall in the den—managed to use her legs and feet to pull the table toward her and get the keys; however, Hendy noticed her efforts and a fight ensued. Vigil was able to free herself while Hendy beat her and even after being hit in the head with a lamp, Vigil managed to stab Hendy in the back of the neck with an icepick she found on the floor. When Hendy fell to the ground, Vigil escaped the house naked save for an iron slave collar and padlocked chains, and began to run down Bass Road in Elephant Butte. Since she had just been taken three days ago, Vigil had not been taken out to the toy box yet.

Vigil was spotted by a couple of passing motorists who did not know what to make of the woman and didn't stop. Vigil finally surprised a woman at home in her trailer watching television who called the police for her. Vigil was then taken to the Sierra Vista

County Hospital emergency room where the chains were cut off and her battered body was cared for.

When police went to Ray's home, they found bloodied sheets in one bedroom with a broken lamp and broken window, thus corroborating Vigil's claims. A pulley device with hooks and chains was mounted on the ceiling and there was a long, coffin-like box along the side of the bed. Large sex toys were on the dresser.

Arrest and Investigation

After Vigil's escape, Ray and Hendy were arrested off Springfield Road in his red Toyota camper. They claimed that they had kidnapped Vigil in an effort to break her of her heroin addiction. Ray and Hendy were taken to nearby Truth or Consequences—formerly Hot Springs—New Mexico and housed in the Cooper Police Training Center.

Both Ray and Hendy were charged with 12 counts consisting of aggravated kidnapping, conspiracy, and aggravated battery and held on $1 million bail.

Soon after Ray was arrested, New Mexico State Police took the case over from the Truth or Consequences Police Department and Agent Wesley LaCuesta—a five-year veteran of the Criminal Assault and Violent Crimes Division—was called on to assist in the investigation. He left his Las Cruces office and headed north to Truth or Consequences.

LaCuesta interviewed Vigil at the hospital. He observed many small cuts on her extremities, injuries to her breasts, welts on her back, and evidence of her being handcuffed.

By early April 1999, over 100 New Mexico State Police and FBI agents were all over Ray's property looking for human remains.

Eleven days after his arrest, Patty Rust committed suicide after assisting law enforcement personnel with detailed drawings of the toy box over the course of four days. Prosecutor Jim Yontz wondered why the FBI would send a woman into a torture chamber where many women had likely been frightened to death by Ray and the torture he inflicted upon them. He then went to visit the toy box. Inside he found a ghastly collection of sex toys, medical devices, whips, clamps, chains, pulleys, rods, saws, and other items for bondage and sadomasochism; in addition to detailed drawings of how Ray liked to torture his victims, medical books on the female anatomy, and, perhaps most damning, a videotape dating back to 1993 showing a woman being tortured.

There was also a television monitor in the right corner of the toy box so Ray's victims could see what he was doing to them if they looked at the monitor while they were secured to the table. He also had a video camera focused upon the table recording everything he was doing. Photographs of the torture he had inflicted upon prior victims decorated the walls, as well as a bunch of dolls which were "strung up in various states of bondage and torture." In addition to the medical texts, Ray had a copy of Brett Easton Ellis' *American Psycho*; a novel detailing violent assaults inflicted by a man when he needed to release steam from his high-stress life that was also made into a film starring Christian Bale. The novel contains very disturbing descriptions of torture. It was presumed that Ray compared himself to the "protagonist" in the novel as he saw himself as in control and his victims as "expendable pawns in his game", even going so far as to call his victims "packages."

With respect to the videotape depicting the torture of one of Ray's victims, the police were able to find the woman on the tape: Kelly Garrett, who had been married mere days before being abducted by Ray and Hendy. Garrett had been held hostage, raped, and tortured for three days before being drugged and left on the side of the road not far from her in-laws' house. Believing Garrett had been out on a drug binge, she was asked to leave and subsequently moved back to Colorado. Investigators found her in Colorado and she stated that she had amnesia for a long time, only recently—as in the past year—remembering what Ray and Hendy had done to her.

The publicity surrounding the case prompted another victim to come forward with her story. Angelica Montano recounted her ordeal at Ray's hands just one month ago.

Angelica Montano

Montano said that she was a casual acquaintance of both Ray and Hendy and had gone to their house on 17 February 1999, looking to borrow cake mix. She said that Ray left the room and then returned with a knife and told her that she was being kidnapped. When Montano looked over at Hendy, she saw the woman holding a gun, pointed at her. She knew they were serious.

Montano said that the couple grabbed, bound, and stripped her before strapping her to a bed and placing a metal collar on her. She said they then attached electrodes to her breasts and shocked her multiple times in addition to "abus[ing] her with various sexual implements." She then said that Ray forced her to give him oral sex.

After having been chained naked to the bed for three days and being subjected to sexual abuse, it was time for Montano to visit the toy box. Ray removed her handcuffs and led her to the bathroom with a long metal leash attached to the dog collar. He bathed her "like a dog, with a chain and everything" Montano would later say. When she was clean, Hendy applied makeup to her face and then draped a robe over her captive's shoulders before Ray and Hendy led her out into the trailer.

In the smaller trailer—the toy box—Montano was strapped to a gynecologist table where she was subjected to additional electric shocks to her genitalia as well as other instances of sexual assault. She said that she repeatedly begged Ray and Hendy to release her and on the fourth day they relented. She was drugged and taken miles away from Ray's property and dumped on a local highway in the desert where a police officer found her.

Even though Montano did, in fact, report the incident to the police, there had been no follow up. When she saw that Ray and Hendy had been arrested, Montano contacted the police again.

Accomplices

In addition to Hendy, investigators discovered two other accomplices: Ray's daughter Glenda Jean "Jesse" Ray; and Dennis Roy Yancy. Yancy and Hendy had dated in the past.

Yancy admitted to strangling Marie Parker—a former girlfriend—after Ray kidnapped and tortured her. Ray videotaped the murder. Yancy also confessed to seeing photographs of one of Ray's ex-wives in various bondage positions as well as watching Ray torture a woman inside the toy box but that he thought it was consensual. Yancy was subsequently convicted of second-degree murder and conspiracy to commit first-degree murder. He received two 15-year sentences. Jesse was also tried and convicted of kidnapping for sexual torture. She was sentenced to seven years and served three, the rest of the time she was on parole.

Hendy was charged with 25 felonies and was looking at 197 years in prison. To save herself, she agreed to plead no contest and testify against Ray and Yancy in exchange for five felony counts and a 36-year sentence. In the Seventh District Court of New Mexico Hendy pled guilty to two counts of first-degree kidnapping for Vigil and Montano, two counts of sexual penetration (rape) in the second degree for the two women, and one count of conspiracy to commit second-degree kidnapping.

Over 100 FBI agents were sent to search Ray's property but they were unable to identify any human remains. Several bones were located but they proved to be of animal origin. Collecting evidence from Ray's home and toy box proved daunting due to the sheer number of items he had amassed for his tortuous pleasure. In one interview, New Mexico Public Safety Director Darren White told reporters that the evidence inside the toy box was "very disturbing stuff" and "literally made my stomach turn."

It was later discovered that Ray would drug his victims with sodium pentothal and phenobarbital to induce amnesia to prevent them from being able to report what had happened to them when they were released. In Kelly Garrett's case, she was unsure about her own recollections of the torture and accompanying nightmares; that is, until the FBI contacted her and, soon thereafter, she was able to remember—in vivid detail—what Ray did to her so she could testify against him in court.

In his recording, Ray described his whole philosophy about drugging his victims and why getting an accurate body count of those victims he killed is impossible. Ray said:

*"If I killed every b*tch that we kidnapped, there'd be bodies strung all over the country. And besides, I don't like killin' a girl, unless it is absolutely necessary. So I've devised a safe, alternate method of disposal. I had plenty of b*tches to practice on over the years, so I've pretty well got it down pat. And I enjoy doin' it. I get off on mind games. After we get completely through with you, you're gonna be drugged up real heavy, with a combination of Sodium Pentothal and Phenobarbital. They are both hypnotic drugs that will make you extremely susceptible to hypnosis, autohypnosis and hypnotic suggestion. You're gonna be kept drugged a couple of days, while I play with your mind. By the time I get through brainwashing you, you're not gonna remember a fu*kin' thing about this little adventure. You won't remember this place, us, or what has happened to you. There won't be any DNA evidence, because you'll be bathed, and both holes between your legs will be thoroughly flushed out. You'll be dressed, sedated, and turned loose on some country road, bruised, heh, sore all over, but nothing that won't heal up in a week or two. The thought of being brainwashed may not be appealing to you, but we been doin' it a long time and it works. And it's the lesser of two evils. I'm sure that you would prefer that, in lieu of being strangled or having your throat cut."*

One can only imagine the pure horror coursing through his victims' minds as they lay, chained atop his torture table, hearing—in very graphic detail—about what they will be enduring.

Trials and Convictions

The press jumped all over the case and soon discovered that everyone who seemingly knew Ray said that he seemed like a "regular" guy. He did not have any criminal record, nor were there any reports about potentially suspicious activities on his property which he leased from the park service. However, reports from the police indicated that he was considerably worse and darker than he initially seemed.

State District Judge Neil Mertz decided that Ray would undergo three separate trials: for Cynthia Vigil, for Angelica Montano, and for Kelly Garrett. The Vigil trial was set to start on 28 March 2000, in Tierra Amarilla. Judge Mertz suppressed Ray's early interviews with the New Mexico State Police and FBI and also banned the media from the voir dire. Just after jury selection, Ray allegedly suffered a heart attack and was taken to a hospital in Las Cruces. The judge postponed the trial for another week and then there were additional delays and several FBI expert witnesses were excluded.

Then, unexpectedly, Judge Mertz decided to start Garrett's trial for her 1996 kidnapping and torture even though it was the weakest case, evidence-wise. Nevertheless, Judge Mertz scheduled it for the end of May. Of course, Ray was pleased with the delays, not to mention Judge Mertz's exclusion of Ray's printed sheet of procedures for handling his slaves as well as all devices found in the trailer for Garrett's trial since nobody could prove they were there in 1996. This left the prosecution with the videotape and the victim's testimony.

When Vigil's trial was actually conducted, it ended in a mistrial because some jurors were not convinced that the women were completely held against their will and there was a subsequent retrial that resulted in convictions for all 12 counts with which Ray was charged.

Montano's trial was delayed indefinitely because, unfortunately, she was rushed to an Albuquerque hospital on 7 May 2001 with pneumonia where she died an hour later from heart failure. She was only 28 years old. As she was one of only three living, known witnesses who were going to testify against Ray, Montano's death dealt a huge blow to the prosecution. However, prosecutor Jim Yontz was prepared to try Ray for Montano's kidnapping and torture by utilizing videotaped statements she had made at a preliminary hearing on 15 and 16 April 1999.

When prosecutors started "closing in" on his daughter Jesse who assisted with some of Ray's earlier kidnappings, Ray decided to take a plea bargain. He received a sentence of 224 years in prison.

Ray suffered a fatal heart attack while incarcerated at Lea County Correctional Facility in Hobbs, New Mexico, on 28 May 2002.

Aftermath

Yancy was paroled in 2010 after serving 11 years of his sentence; however, his release was delayed because of difficulties stemming from his parole plan which had to be established before release. Three months after he was released in 2011, he was charged with violating his parole and subsequently returned to prison and required to serve his entire sentence until 2021.

Ray is suspected of murdering his one-time business partner, Billy Bowers. The two men bought, restored, and sold cars. On 22 September 1988, Bowers disappeared and his family immediately offered a $5,000 reward for any information leading to his safe return. On 28 September 1989, a fisherman found a male body floating in McCrea Canyon which is along the eastern shore of Elephant Butte Lake. The body was wrapped in a blue tarp and secured to two heavy boat anchors. It had a single bullet hole to the head and $49.47 in a pocket but no identification. There were no missing persons reports for a five-foot-ten-inch male in his late-30's or early-40's so the John Doe remained unidentified for over a decade until Cindy Hendy told police that Ray had murdered Bowers. Hendy admitted that Ray confessed the murder to her and told her that since then he had learned to open the victims' stomachs so they would "stay down" when submerged in water and not float to the surface as was the case with Bowers.

When the body was exhumed and dental records compared, the John Doe was, in fact, Bowers. His son Michael was able to retrieve the body of his long-lost father for a proper burial and some closure.

In November 2002, state police officially opened the toy box to the public in the hopes that renewed media attention might help identify additional victims. Inside were signs that said "Satan's Den" and "Bondage Room." The obstetrical table was still there with all of its clamps, leg stretchers, electric wires, chains, and straps. A steel cabinet held numerous surgical instruments and the coffin-shaped box used to terrorize and contain victims was nearby. Ray's meticulous records detailing what he did to his victims was also available. To ensure that none of his victims escaped, Ray had devised an elaborate alarm system and had written instructions to ensure that all straps were secure prior to leaving the toy box.

However, with Ray dead, the investigation went cold, especially since no bodies were ever found, no possible victims were identified, and no suspicious deaths which might have been loosely linked to Ray were solved. Despite the lack of any dead bodies, he is oft-labeled in numerous sources of literature as a serial killer.

According to Jim Fielder in his 2003 book *Slow Death*, both Vigil and Garrett went on to form relationships and start families of their own.

As recently as 2012, additional evidence has been uncovered which indicated there may be additional victims.

THE AMITYVILLE MURDERS

ANA BENSON

Amityville, Long Island became famous with the release of the book called *The Amityville Horror*. Even though the supernatural events described in that book were later on proved to be completely fictional, they inspired numerous Hollywood blockbuster movies that have been popular for decades now. As a society, we love the tales of the unexplained nature and placing them in a very sinister settings adds to the general eerie feeling that attracts the public.

This quiet suburban street looks like a normal New York suburb but Lutz family who were the main characters in *The Amityville Horror* book went through hell in their newly purchased dream home. The said house has a tragic history and Lutz family supposedly experienced it first hand. Yes, it was confirmed that the book featured plenty of false accounts and recollections, but it helped put Amityville on the map and the story soon became well-known throughout the United States and the rest of the world.

However, not all scary stories are made up and there has to be something to them, right? The real events that occurred on a cold autumn day in November of 1974 at a lovely house on 112 Ocean Avenue were as chilling as the most intense work of fiction out there. So let's take a closer look at the actual Amityville horror and discover what really happened in that small town on Long Island.

The DeFeo Family

Ronald Joseph DeFeo, or Big Ronnie as his friends used to call him, married Louise Brigante. Both of them didn't have an easy life and had to struggle quite a lot in their youth. But they did manage to find true happiness with each other and start a family that will slowly grow over the years. Their first son Ronald Joseph DeFeo Jr. was born in 1951. He had a tough time growing up and was physically abused by his peers for being overweight. His nickname was Butch.

Soon enough Ronald DeFeo became an older brother to Dawn Theresa DeFeo. She was born in 1956. Allison Louise DeFeo followed in 1961 so Butch had two sisters now. His new brother Marc Gregory

DeFeo was born in 1962. As you can see, the DeFeos were a normal middle-class family with a lot of children. But there were some issues between the parents after the birth of Marc Gregory and they were separated for a shorter period of time. Ronald did his best to get Louise back and he succeeded.

They moved into the house on 112 Ocean Avenue in the summer of 1965 after purchasing it from the Rileys. Since DeFeos had four children with the fifth one on the way, they needed a large house that will provide them with plenty of space. Big Ronnie worked for a car dealership, and he knew that the price tag for this house will be quite high. Even though he didn't get along with his in-laws before, Big Ronnie asked the Brigante side of the family for financial help and they stepped up. After all, they were living in an apartment in Brooklyn that simply wasn't large enough for this family.

The house itself looked impressive. It was built in 1925 and had amazing details that were very popular for that time, including two windows overlooking the front lawn which will become iconic later on. The design was Dutch colonial and the structure was towering and large. The house had a boathouse as well. DeFeos added various little decorations to the surrounding property over the years and the lawn was tastefully filled with a couple of figurines and water features.

The youngest one, John Matthew DeFeo was born in the autumn of 1965. The life at Amityville seemed quiet and contempt. The children adapted well and life seemed to be improving for the DeFeos. The house became DeFeos real home, but things will change very quickly.

The terrifying murder

The autumns in Amityville are cozy and pleasant. The locals enjoy it a lot and they tend to go out during the day. When the night comes, they find a nice bar or a restaurant to spend an evening with the friends. Henry's Bar is located on the Ocean Avenue and it was one of the hot spots back in the day. The nearby residents frequented that place and the atmosphere was warm and welcoming.

However, on the evening of November the 13th, 1974 the people at Henry's Bar were astonished when Ronald DeFeo Jr. burst through the front door screaming and shouting: "You got to help me! I think my mother and father are shot." He then started to weep and cry after he fell to the ground. Everyone jumped from their seats and ran out in order to get to the DeFeo house as fast as possible. Their assumption was that an outsider attacked this large family and they had no idea what to expect. They got into a single car with DeFeo in the backseat and rushed down the street towards the house. From this moment on nothing in Amityville, Long Island will be the same.

Bobby Kelske was Ronald's best friend and he was the driver of the car. They arrived in front of the house quickly and Bobby led the way into the DeFeo home. The front door was unlocked and the only sound coming from the inside was the barking of the family dog who was tied up inside the kitchen area. Bobby climbed the stairs and found his way to the master bedroom where he stumbled upon a terrible scene. Both Ronald DeFeo Sr. and Louise DeFeo laid in the double bed with visible gunshots. They were on their stomachs and the wounds and blood were very prominent even in this dimly lit room. Bobby felt sick and the rest of the guys carried him out.

One man remained in the house, searching for the remaining members of DeFeo family. He entered another bedroom which belonged to the two younger brothers. Both of them were positioned in the same manner as their parents – on their stomach with gunshot wounds. It was clear to him that they were dead for quite some time now because the blood started to clot and darken.

He quickly returned to the ground floor where the rest of the guys including Ronald DeFeo Jr. stood. It didn't take them too long to decide to call the police and tell them what happened. The law enforcement acted quickly and they were at the DeFeo house in no time. The police officer who arrived first searched the rest of the house and found additional two victims, Dawn and Allison DeFeo.

The police issued a press release where they pointed out the fact that all of the victims were shot in the same way – with a bullet through their backs with the exemption of the parents who were shot twice. It appeared that all of them were asleep when this crime happened but it was later discovered that the girls were actually awake.

With that said, it was clear that the police had a lot of work to do. After all, they had six victims on their hands and had no idea who might be behind this. They took Ronald DeFeo Jr. to the police station in order to keep him safe because they suspected he might be the next target. DeFeo Jr. told them a story about a mob hitman who was probably the main perpetrator of these murders. They also had to take a written statement from him and learn as much as they could about this alleged hitman. However, this is when things got murky and the police realized that Ronald DeFeo Jr. might be the actual killer.

The interrogation and arrest

Since the first officer arrived to the crime scene quickly, he was able to do the research properly without too much contamination. He was greeted by the group of men standing on the front lawn around the crying Ronald who was in a state of shock. He refused to escort the police officer into the house and claimed he didn't want to see his family dead. Ronald DeFeo Jr. seemed to be in great distress and scared for his own life but he did reenter the house and sat at the kitchen table eventually.

The police officer inspected the bedrooms and called for a backup. Soon enough detectives arrived and the media followed them. Gasper Randazzo was the detective who questioned Ronald DeFeo Jr. in the kitchen and he listened to his account of the events that happened that day. Ronald claimed that he was out of the house since the morning, working at the car dealership. He arrived at the house in the afternoon and discovered the bodies of his family members. Ronald even told a name of a suspect to the police.

Apparently, Louis Falini, a well-known criminal with the ties to the local mafia and organized crime murdered the DeFeos and now Ronald was scared for his own life too. Another detective made a suggestion that Ronald should be placed in the protective custody until they catch Falini and take him off the streets. DeFeo Jr. was driven to the police station, leaving the detectives to do their crime scene investigation in the house where this tragic mass murder occurred.

After arriving at the Fourth Precinct, Ronald DeFeo Jr. was questioned in more details. He provided the police with more information about Falini and his supposed connection to the family. DeFeo Jr. said that Falini lived with them in the house on 112 Ocean Avenue a couple of years back. He knew the layout perfectly and was familiar with all the valuables DeFeos had inside. As a matter of fact, DeFeo Jr. said that the robbery was the motivation for this crime since DeFeos had a small gem collection hidden in their basement, and some cash as well.

DeFeo Jr. started to open up slowly while still remaining visibly nervous and overall scared. It was clear to the detectives that he was in some sort of panic but they weren't sure if it was due to the fact that the mafia hitman was possibly targeting him, or because he actually committed the murders. Police were not completely certain that his recollection of the events was completely accurate at this point. After a couple of hours of conversation, the detectives left DeFeo Jr. to sleep at the station while they returned to the house in order to assist their colleagues with the evidence collection.

The evidence at the house

Some major discoveries were happening at the house while the detectives were talking to DeFeo Jr. at the police station. The first clue that he might not be that truthful were boxes of ammunition which were found hidden inside of his bedroom. The .35 caliber bullets were a perfect match to the murder weapon and the wounds. The police officers were told by the family friends and neighbors who were gathering in front of the house that Big Ronnie was a huge fan of guns and had a couple of them inside the house.

It was clear to them that the gun which was used for these murders came from the house and not from a mafia hitman. DeFeo Jr.'s story started collapsing and the detectives knew that the culprit was back at the police station sleeping. When the morning came, the detectives entered the room where DeFeo Jr. slept and started reading him his rights. He still insisted that the mafia hitman should be their person of interest and that he had nothing to do with these murders.

He started to change his story, claiming that he was actually threatened by Falini and that he was at the house when the murders happened. As a matter of fact, Falini took him to each and every room as he murdered the rest of the DeFeo family as they slept. Butch was there and witnessed everything. The detectives knew that his story was crumbling down and were pretty sure they got the right guy.

Butch even added the unlikely detail about the weapon disposal somewhere in the neighboring Brooklyn. The list of things that simply didn't add up kept piling up and the detectives simply waited for the moment when DeFeo Jr. will stop lying and tell them what actually happened. After a couple of minutes, DeFeo Jr. cracked and confessed to everything by saying: "Once I started, I just couldn't stop. It went so fast."

DeFeo Jr. provided the police with additional information about the exact timeline of the murders, what he did with the murder weapon and told them he cleaned himself up after the crime in order to appear completely normal at his work place. He throw away the stained clothes as well. The case against him was as solid as a rock and police had no reason to suspect that the mafia hitman Falini had anything to do with this mass murder. As a matter of fact, Falini was out of the state at the time which gave him an ironclad alibi.

The crime scene analysis

Even though the police had a very solid case against Ronald DeFeo Jr. there were still a couple of burning questions that needed to be answered before the actual trial started. Butch confessed that he did work alone, but the time between the murders puzzled the police. Surely, someone must have heard something and woken up. It was simply impossible to murder six people in the same manner within minutes without anyone registering the gunshots. The detectives wondered if Ronald DeFeo Jr. had some outside help.

The rifle which was the murder weapon was fairy loud and a silencer didn't muffle the sound. The neighborhood itself didn't notice any gunshots. Since the murders were committed in the early hours, the majority of them were asleep which might be the reason. However, the people who were awake at that time only noticed the dog who was barking in the kitchen. Everything else was silent.

It was obvious that the murders happened within a very small time frame. The bodies were examined and the blood samples didn't show any medications in their systems. None of the members of the family were drugged and sedated which lead the police to assume that someone must have woken up while the murderer was on the loose. It was later discovered that the girls did wake up and they were aware that something was going on in the house. It seems that they decided to lay in their beds, pretending to be asleep.

DeFeo Jr. moved through the house, killing each and every family member while they were in their beds. He exited the home afterwards, looking as his usual self and managing to suppress what happened in order to appear normal before he raised the alarm which got everyone on their feet. It was obvious that he had some kind of mental disorder because not everyone is capable of ignoring the mass murder and going through their day as if nothing significant had happened.

The trial and the background of Ronald DeFeo Jr.

The trial of Ronald DeFeo Jr. started almost exactly one year after the murders. His defense relied heavily on the insanity claims and Dr.

Daniel Schwartz supported it. He was brought into this case after the leading attorney on DeFeo's team invited him to examine Ronald and provide his expert opinion. DeFeo Jr. told the psychiatrist that he was hearing voices and that the murders were committed in self-defense.

Prosecution had their own expert who debunked the defense's claims. Dr. Harold Zolan presented the courtroom with his psychiatric analysis of Ronald DeFeo Jr. and told everyone that Butch suffered from antisocial personality disorder which was intensified by his excessive hallucinogens and opiate use. Ronald DeFeo Jr. did often indulge in LSD and heroin, making his existing personality disorder even more dangerous and severe. Dr. Zolan tore down the defense's strategy by stating that Ronald DeFeo Jr. was completely aware of his actions and that he was sane. There were no voices in his head and his mind was completely clear at the time of the murders.

So what prompted the defense to try and claim insanity on the behalf of their client? After the arrest, the police started uncovering various details from the private lives of the DeFeos. The family seemed idyllic from afar but things were not as perfect as they appeared to be. Ronald DeFeo Sr. or Big Ronnie as his friends called him, was abusive to both his wife and his children. Ronald DeFeo Jr. was often the target of these aggressive outbursts, mostly because he was the oldest of the children and he expected much more from him.

Ronald DeFeo Jr. was an overweight child who was bullied by his peers in school. It had a huge impact on his overall academic performance and his personality seemed to change gradually. He started to become more introverted and avoided hanging out with his friends and neighbors. He did manage to shed some weight but he also became pretty aggressive to his father. He would often talk back to him and even physically attack Ronald DeFeo Sr. His mother was very concerned and Ronald Jr. was sent to a psychiatrist in order to get some counseling and try to resolve his anger issues. This was all taking place when Ronald Jr. was only fifteen years old.

Since DeFeo family did have money, Ronald Jr. started spending it on heroin and LSD. He was seventeen when the teachers at his school noticed that Butch was acting violently to his classmates and he was quickly expelled. It is unknown if the school also knew about his heavy drug use. The DeFeos tried to ignore the fact that their eldest son was a failure and they bought him expensive presents despite of his behavior. They were doing everything in order to please him but nothing seemed to lessen his aggression.

When Ronald DeFeo Jr. was eighteen, his father gave him a job at the family car dealership. He didn't have the proper background to do the work well, but he was accepted without any questions. Butch continued to spend his money on firearm and drugs. He would occasionally binge on alcohol as well. His behavior was getting out of control but it looked like the parents decided to turned their heads away and ignore the situation that was unravelling right there in front of them.

One family friend recalled an event that occurred during one of the fights between Louise and Ronald DeFeo Sr. when Ronald Jr. threatened his father with a gun and actually pulled the trigger but nothing happened. It looked like the gun was broken. DeFeo Sr. was left in shock which eventually ended the fight. The fact that Ronald Jr. was capable of this could have told them that something big might be on the way.

Butch still wanted more funds from his family so he decided to try and steal the money from the car dealership he worked at. His planning was meticulous and he found a friend who would help him. Staging a robbery is not an easy task and that speaks volumes about Butch's mental state. He knew what he was doing and was aware of the consequences. Eventually, his plans did fail and he was taken to the police station in order to provide them with the sketch of his assailant. He refused and the case was dropped. Ronald DeFeo Sr. was very angry with his son and he wanted to get the information about this event from him right away. DeFeo Jr. told his father to leave him alone or he will kill him.

There were so many red flags before the actual murder so we are left wondering if it could have been prevented. It was clear that Ronald DeFeo Jr. had issues and his behavior was very strange but the claim that he was insane simply couldn't be supported by the experts. He was in his right mind when he committed these murders and the very fact that he managed to clean himself up and go to work tells a lot about premeditation and preparation.

Yes, he did have a tough childhood and he was bullied both at home and at school. His aggressive personality started to emerge as he got older and the heavy drug use simply wasn't helping him at all. Ronald DeFeo Jr. fits the description of the antisocial personality disorder sufferer to the smallest details. He is a sociopath but he is definitely not hearing voices and the defense simply couldn't sell that story in the courtroom.

Ronald DeFeo Jr. was found guilty of these murders on November 21, 1975 so the trial itself was very short. He was responsible for six second-degree murders and the actual sentencing came a couple of weeks later. The judge gave him six sentences of 25 years to life. The motive itself was never determined. However, Ronald Jr. continued his fight to prove his innocence and gave a couple of different recollections of the night of the crime in the years to come. He often talked to the media who helped him get the word out.

Post-conviction interviews and appeals

This case became notorious after the release of the book called *The Amityville Horror*. The public was familiar with the basics of this case and they wanted to know more about the murders. The media followed the story so Ronald DeFeo Jr. managed to give plenty of interviews to the press in which he claimed to be innocent.

He completely changed his story in one interview which was conducted in 1986. He blamed his sister Dawn for shooting their father first. Their mother then murdered all of the children before finally turning to Ronald Jr. who killed her in self-defense. An alternative story emerged in 1990 when Ronald Jr. tried to get an early release from the prison. He added the second assailant into the storyline claiming that a stranger assisted Dawn with the murders. As Dawn was the last person standing, Ronald Jr. attacked her after finding out what she had done and accidentally shot her with the rifle.

Butch then presented the authorities with the girl called Geraldine who was supposedly his wife at the time of the murders. He said that he moved in with her a couple of months back and that they lived together in New Jersey, far away from the DeFeo house. His frightened mother called him one day prior to the murders asking him for help because Dawn was fighting with their father. Since he was an obedient son, he went to Amityville in order to help make things right.

In another version of the story, Butch claimed that he stayed in New Jersey with his wife and her brother at the time of the murders. He then visited the house after a long day at work and discovered the bodies of his family. The law enforcement took these claims seriously and decided to investigate the said wife and the brother properly just to confirm that they had the right person behind the bars.

They quickly uncovered the truth behind Geraldine and her sibling. Geraldine lived in a completely different city in the northern New York at the time of the murders and she was actually married to another man. Butch provided the police with the name of Geraldine's brother but it was soon revealed that the man didn't even exist. Geraldine wasn't one of the witnesses for 440 motion hearing because the police already debunked all of her claims. Butch DeFeo's appeal was thrown out once again.

Ronald DeFeo Jr. was placed in Greenhaven correctional Facility, New York immediately after the sentencing and he remains there to this day. He continued to accept the interview requests which seem to spike after each new movie release inspired by the actual events which happened on 112 Ocean Avenue. Various media covered the real murders and there are numerous books and documentaries about this case.

It still remains as one of the most mysterious crimes because Ronald DeFeo Jr. never gave the actual reason behind the murders. The police did suspect that he was motivated by the life insurance money he would get after the death of his father. They later abandoned their initial thoughts. Ronald DeFeo Jr.'s appeals have all been turned down and it looks like he will not get out of the prison anytime soon.